SOMEONE WHO BECKONS

Readings and Prayers for 60 Days

TIMOTHY DUDLEY-SMITH

InterVarsity Press
Downers Grove
Illinois 60515

To Ronald Inchley

with affection
and admiration

© *Timothy Dudley-Smith 1978*
First American printing, December 1978, by
InterVarsity Press with permission from
Universities and Colleges Christian Fellowship,
Leicester, England.

InterVarsity Press is the book-publishing division
of Inter-Varsity Christian Fellowship, a
student movement active on campus at hundreds
of universities, colleges and schools of
nursing. For information about local and regional
activities, write IVCF, 233 Langdon St.,
Madison, WI 53703.

Distributed in Canada through
InterVarsity Press, 1875 Leslie St., Unit 10,
Don Mills, Ontario M3B 2M5, Canada.

ISBN 0-87784-731-2
Library of Congress Catalog Card
Number: 78-18548

Printed in the United States of America

CONTENTS

Sources and acknowledgments

The Bible text in this publication is from the Revised Standard Version, copyrighted 1946, 1952, © 1971, 1973 by the Division of Christian Education, National Council of the Churches of Christ in the United States of America, and used by permission.

The author is grateful for permission to quote those of the following works that are in copyright.

1. D. R. Davies, *In search of myself* (Geoffrey Bles, 1961), pp. 189f.
2. 'Putting in the seed,' from *The Poetry of Robert Frost*, edited by Edward Connery Lathem. (Copyright 1916, © 1969, by Holt, Rinehart and Winston. Copyright 1944 by Robert Frost. Reprinted by permission of Holt, Rinehart and Winston, Publishers.)
3. Bernard Lord Manning, *The hymns of Wesley and Watts* (Epworth, 1942), pp. 28f.
4. Joy Davidman, *Smoke on the mountain.* (Copyright © 1953, 1954, by Joy Davidman. Used by permission of the Westminster Press.)
5. J. S. Whale, *Christian doctrine* (Cambridge University Press, 1950), pp. 186f.
6. John Baillie, *Invitation to pilgrimage* (Oxford University Press, 1942), pp. 115f., reprinted by permission of the Oxford University Press.
7. John Newton. 'A thought on the seashore,' in *The Olney hymns,* collection of 1779.
8. G. K. Chesterton, *Orthodoxy* (Dodd, Mead & Company, 1974.)
9. 'The two children,' *The complete poems of W. H. Davies.* (Copyright © 1963 by Jonathan Cape Ltd. Reprinted by permission of Wesleyan University Press.)
10. Richard Chenivix Trench, 'God our refuge.'
11. Laurens Van der Post, *Venture to the interior.* (William Morrow & Co., Inc., 1973.)
12. Derek Kidner, *A time to mourn, and a time to dance* (InterVarsity Press, 1976), pp. 101f.
13. J. S. Reynolds, *Canon Christopher* (The Abbey Press, Abingdon, 1967), pp. 13f.
14. G. L. Heawood, *Vacant possession* (SCM Press, 1951), pp. 121-23.

15. Bruce Kenrick, *Come out the wilderness* (Collins, 1962; Fontana, 1970), pp. 162f.
16. F. R. Barry, *Mervyn Haigh* (SPCK, 1964), pp. 22f.
17. Michael Burns, *Mr Lyward's answer* (Hamish Hamilton, 1956), pp. 276f., copyright © 1965 Michael Burns, Hamish Hamilton, Ltd., London.
18. Isak Dinesen, *Out of Africa.* (Random House, Inc., 1972.)
19. The Lady Julian of Norwich, *The revelation of divine love*, translated by James Walsh (Anthony Clarke Books, 1973), p. 116.
20. Handley C. G. Moule, *Charles Simeon* (Methuen, 1892), p. 72.
21. F. Pratt Green (1903-   ), 'Here, Master, in this quiet place,' by permission of Oxford University Press.
22. Florence M. G. Higham, *Lord Shaftesbury* (SCM Press, 1945), pp. 7f.
23. Dorothy L. Sayers, from the Introduction to *The Man to be King* (Gollancz, 1946), pp. 22f.
24. 'Easter night,' *The poems of Alice Meynell* (Hollis and Carter, 1947); and 'Easter Day,' by Henry Vaughan.
25. John Greenleaf Whittier, 'To a young physician, with Doré's picture of Christ healing the sick.'
26. J. B. Lancelot, *Francis James Chavasse* (Basil Blackwell, 1929), pp. 51f.
27. John R. W. Stott, *Who Is My Neighbor?* (InterVarsity Press, 1975), pp. 18-19.
28. Patricia St John, 'The Alchemist,' *Verses* (CSSM, 1953).
29. Ronald S. Wallace, *Many things in parables* (Oliver and Boyd, 1955), p. 78.
30. Helmut Thielieke, *The waiting Father*. (Harper & Row, Publishers, Inc.)
31. John Henry Newman, *Apologia pro vita sua* (Note A), (1863), pp. 192f.
32. O. Hallesby, *Prayer* (Augsburg, 1948).
33. Francis Schaeffer, *The God who is there* (InterVarsity Press, 1968), pp. 133f.
34. P. Carnegie Simpson, *The fact of Christ* (Hodder and Stoughton, 1903), pp. 29f.
35. W. Haslam, *From death to life* (Marshall, Morgan and Scott, undated, c. 1870), pp. 47f.
36. Helen Lee, *The growing years* (Falcon, 1963), pp. 133f.
37. Paul Tournier, *A doctor's casebook in the light of the Bible.* (Harper & Row, Publishers, Inc.)
38. William Temple, *Readings in St John's Gospel* (Macmillan, 1949), pp. 384f., reprinted by permission of Macmillan, London and Basingstoke.
39. David Winter, *Hereafter* (Hodder and Stoughton, 1972), pp. 62f.
40. Marcus Loane, *Masters of the English Reformation* (Church Book Room Press, 1954), p. 236.
41. W. E. Sangster, *The secret of radiant life.* (Copyright © 1957 by Abingdon Press. Used by permission.)
42. H. R. Rookmaaker, *Modern art and the death of a culture* (InterVarsity Press, 1970), pp. 46f.
43. James S. Stewart, *A faith to proclaim.* (Baker Book House, reprinted 1972.)
44. William Barclay, *Jesus as they saw him* (SCM Press, 1962), pp. 428f.
45. John C. Pollock, *A Cambridge movement* (John Murray [Publishers], Ltd. 1953), p. 70.
46. Dr and Mrs Howard Taylor, *Hudson Taylor: the growth of a soul* (Marshall, Morgan and Scott, 1911), p. 129.
47. C. S. Lewis, *The last battle.* (Reprinted with permission of Macmillan Publishing Co., Inc., © 1956 by C. S. Lewis.)
48. C. S. Lewis, *Letters to an American Lady*, edited by C. S. Kilby (Hodder and Stoughton, 1969), p. 114, used by permission of Wm. B. Eerdmans Publishing Co.
49. John Bunyan, *The pilgrim's progress* (1678).
50. Bryan Green, *Saints alive* (Epworth, 1959), pp. 113f.
51. Aubrey Attwater, *A short history of Pembroke College* (Cambridge University Press, 1936), p. 39f.
52. *The memoirs of Sir Thomas Fowell Buxton*, edited by Charles Buxton (Everyman's Library, J. M. Dent, 1925, p. 99.

53. John R. W. Stott, *Understanding the Bible* (Scripture Union, 1972), p. 203.

54. J. B. Phillips, from the Translator's Preface to *Letters to young churches* (Geoffrey Bles, 1947), p. xxii.

55. Handley C. G. Moule, *Charles Simeon* (Methuen, 1892), pp. 14f.

56. T. S. Eliot, *The cocktail party.* (Copyright, 1950, by T. S. Eliot; renewed, 1978, by Esme Valerie Eliot. Reprinted by permission of Harcourt Brace Jovanovich, Inc.)

57. C. S. Lewis, *George MacDonald, an anthology* (Geoffrey Bles, 1946), pp. 103, 113, 127.

58. Rose Macaulay, *The towers of Trebizond* (Collins, 1956; Fontana, 1962), pp. 54f.

59. Thomas Campion, 'Never weather-beaten sail...'

60. Henry Vaughan, 'Peace.'

Finally, I acknowledge with gratitude the help of my former secretary, Miss Grace Jackson: who not only typed the manuscript and read the proofs, but, as she has so often done for me before, brought order out of chaos.

Introduction

Someday, perhaps, when I am quietly reading my newspaper, one of my proleptic grandchildren will come across this book.

'Grandpapa,' he will say, 'Is this yours?'

'Yes.'

'It's got your name on it, Grandpapa. Did you write it?'

'Yes.'

'Why did you write it, Grandpapa?'

'Well, I suppose because someone asked me to ... hadn't you better go and see what your mother is doing in the kitchen?'

'S'all right, Grandpapa, I like it here. Why did they ask you to write it?'

'Well, I think they wanted a book which might help people as they learn to talk to God. They asked me to write down some of the talks I have had with him, and the way what I read shapes the prayers I say.'

'Oh. There are no pictures, Grandpapa.'

'No.'

'That's a pity.'

'Yes, I expect you're right.'

'Is it rather a dull book, Grandpapa?'

'Well, I daresay it is ... I really think Mummy would like you to go and find her.'

'P'raps I'll write a dull book one day, too, Grandpapa. It's quite short, isn't it, and it doesn't look very difficult. I bet I could.'

And one day I daresay he will. Lots of people do.

I have begun with that bit of dialogue, partly so that if there are no pictures there will be at least one conversation, and partly because I send this book to the Publisher (the one who asked me to do it) with much diffidence. I think it may indeed be dull. It looks easy, even where it wasn't – and I distrust that kind of easiness. And can they really help or interest anyone else, this set of 'meditations', spontaneous prayers, arising out of the juxtaposition of a part of Scripture with some fragment from my reading that has appealed to me: some of them simply taken from the ragbag of commonplace books which have been by me since I was a student?

Well, I am told perhaps they can. Certainly any help that we can give one another in this difficult subject of prayer is more than welcome. Intercession is the only theme I was specifically asked to include; and you will see some thoughts about it in the following pages. One reason, perhaps, why I felt I ought not simply to decline the invitation (though I tried to do that) is because I have never myself found prayer easy – or very seldom. 'If you want to shame a Christian,' my first bishop, Christopher Chavasse, said once, 'ask him about his prayers.' You will see from these pages what a beginner I am. Even so, there is much on the debit side which they do not disclose.

A word about the title. It comes, with his permission, from a sermon by Alan Glendining, Rector of Sandringham, preached in Haddiscoe Church at a Thanksgiving Service for Jimmy Broughton, sometime Youth Chaplain in the diocese of Norwich. I have put the complete sentence on the title-page: and I add another from the same sermon (I copied them down on the Order of Service to my neighbour's astonishment): 'Love is not so much a matter of being willing to listen as of wanting to hear.' They both bear thinking about.

I hope (if I may now address you personally), that you won't skim through a few of these at a sitting, say 'How nice!'or 'Pretty thin' or 'It's been done before, and rather better' – and put the book away. If I may suggest, do not look beyond the section you are presently using. Try one a day, not more; perhaps only one a Sunday. There is no particular sequence in the themes I have chosen, and so, after the first, they simply follow the order of the Bible passages. Perhaps I should add, too, that most of these are deliberately familiar. Indeed I have sought, by and large, to stick to known ground. What most of us need is not new Scriptures but new eyes.

Read the verses of the Bible carefully, therefore. Read them, calling to mind all you know about them, and yet at the same time as if you had never set eyes on these words before. Begin with a prayer that God will use these moments to your benefit and blessing. (If you do no more than this, your money will have been well spent). Next read the 'extract', meditating as to why it was chosen, and where it is connected with the Scripture. Then make my prayer your own, slowly and deliberately, in the sight of God. Or rather, *use* my prayer as the raw material, the jumping-off point of a prayer that really is your own. Never mind if you do not always see what I, or the writers I have quoted, are getting at. Not everything, I hope, is on the surface. Some extracts (for example the reference to Narnia) need some knowledge of the background in order to make much sense; others are more obvious, though I think there is only one instance where I have included an actual commentary upon the scripture quoted. Perhaps, indeed, some extracts will whet your appetite for a new author or a new book. I could of course easily have filled this little book with quotations from a single author – for example, J. R. W. Stott or C. S. Lewis – or from the considerable range of Christian books which appear under the same imprint as this one. But I have thought it better to ration my sources in order to gain variety. For the same reason, I have not confined myself to authors whose theology would always necessarily be mine. G. K. Chesterton, for example, has still much to teach us and (especially in his poetry) great power to move us; but I can neither follow nor commend him in his more sectarian enthusiasms. There are some writers here of whom I have to say that I know very little of their other works: and a few of whom I do not know if they profess Christian faith at all. I claim nothing therefore for my 'extracts' than that in them their diverse authors have said something meaningful to me. If, then (*pace* my imaginary grandchild), this is a less dull book than it might have been, my thanks are due to them – and so are yours.

TDS
Ruan Minor
April 1977

1. Someone who beckons

'I am a Jew, born at Tarsus in Cilicia, but brought up in this city at the feet of Gamaliel, educated according to the strict manner of the law of our fathers, being zealous for God as you all are this day. I persecuted this Way to the death, binding and delivering to prison both men and women, as the high priest and the whole council of elders bear me witness. From them I received letters to the brethren, and I journeyed to Damascus to take those also who were there and bring them in bonds to Jerusalem to be punished.

'As I made my journey and drew near to Damascus, about noon a great light from heaven suddenly shone about me. And I fell to the ground and heard a voice saying to me, "Saul, Saul, why do you persecute me?" And I answered, "Who are you, Lord?" And he said to me, "I am Jesus of Nazareth whom you are persecuting." Now those who were with me saw the light but did not hear the voice of the one who was speaking to me. And I said "What shall I do, Lord?" And the Lord said to me, "Rise, and go into Damascus, and there you will be told all that is appointed for you to do." And when I could not see because of the brightness of that light, I was led by the hand by those who were with me, and came into Damascus.*

'And one Ananias, a devout man according to the law, well spoken of by all the Jews who lived there, came to me, and standing by me said to me, "Brother Saul, receive your sight." And in that very hour I received my sight and saw him. And he said, "The God of our fathers appointed you to know his will, to see the Just One and to hear a voice from his mouth; for you will be a witness for him to all men of what you have seen and heard. And now why do you wait? Rise and be baptized, and wash away your sins, calling on his name." '

Acts 22: 3–16

One evening, after supper, I set off in the pouring rain. I took a circular path over fields which ultimately brought me back to my starting-point. From a cloud-laden sky, the rain beat fiercely on to my face, and I felt some kind of savage joy and satisfaction. I suddenly said to myself: 'Why don't you end it all?'

I realized that I was standing with the beach below. It was late. The night was dark, I could hear the waves beating up against the rocks. In a strange excitement I made my way down to the sea, sat on a rock and gazed round. Behind me was a light in a window, and I found myself wondering, as though it did not concern me, whether it was our bungalow. Then I looked out to sea. It was all dark except for the white foam of the waters. Before I realized it, the waves had reached where I sat. Swept by an eerie emotional exaltation, I plunged into the dark waters.

I must have swum, though I am a poor swimmer. Then in a flash, a thunderous flash, I realized what I was doing. 'Good God! What am I doing?' With despairing strength, I swam back. Oh that struggle! I was suspended between life and death!

I felt my feet touch bottom and waded out, out beyond the reach of the tide. I sat down and broke into a convulsion of weeping. Suddenly, unaccountably, there came to my mind—so vividly—a picture of my mother teaching me the catechism from the little book, *Rhodd Mam* (*My Mother's Gift*). It was so powerful and clear. I saw the kitchen and the armchair in which my mother sat. I saw the spectacles half-way down her nose. I saw the little iron stand on which I sat beside her. And I heard her saying—'Who is Jesus Christ?' to which I answered, 'Jesus Christ is my Saviour'. It was just like that. A deep peace, literally 'the peace which the world can neither give nor take away', flooded my entire being. I knew I had passed through the great tribulation. 'Rock of Ages—cleft for *me*—naked come to Thee for dress.' In the final anguish, hovering between life and death, I found myself, as I was, and in my utter nakedness and worthlessness I found God. And finding Him, though this was not realized until later, I found everything.

D. R. Davies

'Who are you, Lord?'
Who are you who remind me,
Sometimes when I least expect it, that
something of eternity is set in every man's heart?
Who are you who speak to me
in persistent if indistinguishable voices,
guilt, nostalgia, heartache, longing?
   I know who you are, of course, Lord:
Jesus of Nazareth, someone who beckons,
calling today as you have always called.
Knocking as you have always knocked.
I know who you are: you are my Saviour, Jesus.
I found you long ago: or rather you found me.
   I know who you are, Lord, nearer than breathing,
closer than hands and feet,
by whose name my sins are washed away
and to whose name I bear my witness
and whom I love.
Beckon me on, then, Jesus my Lord.
Grant me to follow as you lead,
higher up and deeper in.
Beckon me on, and I will follow,
never asking 'Who are you?'
because I know.
Amen.

2. Seeds in springtime

Then God said, 'Let us make man in our image, after our likeness; and let them have dominion over the fish of the sea, and over the birds of the air, and over the cattle, and over all the earth, and over every creeping thing that creeps upon the earth.' So God created man in his own image, in the image of God he created him; male and female he created them. And God blessed them, and God said to them, 'Be fruitful and multiply, and fill the earth and subdue it; and have dominion over the fish of the sea and over the birds of the air and over every living thing that moves upon the earth.' And God said, 'Behold, I have given you every plant yielding seed which is upon the face of all the earth, and every tree with seed in its fruit; you shall have them for food. And to every beast of the earth, and to every bird of the air, and to everything that creeps on the earth, everything that has the breath of life, I have given every green plant for food.' And it was so. And God saw everything that he had made, and behold, it was very good. And there was evening and there was morning, a sixth day.

Genesis 1: 26–31

Putting in the seed

You come to fetch me from my work tonight
When supper's on the table, and we'll see
If I can leave off burying the white
Soft petals fallen from the apple tree
(Soft petals, yes, but not so barren quite,
Mingled with these, smooth bean and wrinkled pea;)
And go along with you ere you lose sight
Of what you came for and become like me,
Slave to a springtime passion for the earth.
How Love burns through the Putting in the Seed
On through the watching for that early birth
When, just as the soil tarnishes with weed,
The sturdy seedling with arched body comes
Shouldering its way and shedding the earth crumbs.

Robert Frost

'Behold, it was very good'—

I can believe it, Lord!
How good it must have been!
And still some of the glory of that
first and new creation
clings
to Mother Earth.
I thank you for Spring: for those
mysterious life-forces in every
sturdy seedling.
I thank you for the principle of life
in all these dry-as-dust granules
as I shake them from the bright packets
into my hand.
And across your world, year by year,
we all feel it: 'Slaves
to a springtime passion for the earth'—
partners, somehow in creation:
filling a role that was ours from the
unspoilt beginning when
Adam
was a gardener.

And this reminds me, Lord, in all my busy days
of desk and paper, telephone and car, meetings
and appointments—
this reminds me that there are depths in all of us
which respond
unexpectedly
along forgotten paths—forgotten, at least, to urban man.
Thank you for the hidden things of your creation,
hidden in nature,
hidden in the earth and in the seed,
hidden in me.
Thank you for yet another Good I take for granted.
Thank you for Adam's blessing which is
mine too.

Amen.

3. Experience of God

The same night he arose and took his two wives, his two maids, and his eleven children, and crossed the ford of the Jabbok. He took them and sent them across the stream, and likewise everything that he had. And Jacob was left alone; and a man wrestled with him until the breaking of the day.

When the man saw that he did not prevail against Jacob, he touched the hollow of his thigh; and Jacob's thigh was put out of joint as he wrestled with him. Then he said, 'Let me go, for the day is breaking.' But Jacob said, 'I will not let you go, unless you bless me.' And he said to him, 'What is your name?' And he said, 'Jacob.'

Then he said, 'Your name shall no more be called Jacob, but Israel, for you have striven with God and with men, and have prevailed.' Then Jacob asked him, 'Tell me, I pray, your name.' But he said, 'Why is it that you ask my name?' And there he blessed him. So Jacob called the name of the place Peniel, saying, 'For I have seen God face to face, and yet my life is preserved.' The sun rose upon him as he passed Penuel, limping because of his thigh.

Genesis 32: 22–31

Most men and women merely disgust us when they talk about their souls and their secret experiences; they did this quite effectually even before psychology became the rage; but Wesley's common sense and scholarly taste kept him from mawkish excesses without crushing his spirit. The result is that few people have been as successful as he was in speaking at once with passion and with decency about God's work in their own lives. For him the important things are the great, external, objective truths about God, the Father, the Son, and the Holy Ghost, and the definite impact of faith in these on his own life and other men's. Through all the book there rings an absolutely overmastering note of confidence, certainty, and happiness. 'The best of all is, God is with us,' with us especially in Emmanuel the incarnate Son: nothing can make Wesley forget that. Historic Christianity, applied to the individual soul and the sharing of this experience with other men who know it too—so Wesley reaches that sense of a common life which all 'real' Christians—Wesley's word—live. So, too, he comes to yearn over the great troubled world that is missing this heavenly treasure.

Lastly, there is something else. There is the solid structure of historic dogma; there is the passionate thrill of present experience; but there is, too, the glory of a mystic sunlight coming directly from another world. This transfigures history and experience. This puts past and present into the timeless eternal now. This brings together God and man until Wesley talks with God as a man talks with his friend. This gives to the hymnbook its divine audacity, those passages only to be understood by such as have sat in heavenly places in Christ Jesus, and being caught up into paradise have heard unspeakable words which it is not lawful for a man to utter.

Bernard Manning

'I will not let you go'—
so said Jacob. 'I will not let you go,
unless you bless me.'
'*Goodnight, God*,' say I (all too often, don't I?).
'*Bless those I love. I must go now. Goodnight.*'
So let Wesley give me words, and may your Spirit
make them mine:

> Come, O thou Traveller unknown,
> Whom still I hold, but cannot see;
> My company before is gone,
> And I am left alone with thee;
> With thee all night I mean to stay,
> And wrestle till the break of day.
>
> I need not tell thee who I am,
> My misery or sin declare;
> Thyself has called me by my name;
> Look on thy hands, and read it there!
> But who, I ask thee, who art thou?
> Tell me thy name, and tell me now.
>
> Yield to me now, for I am weak,
> But confident in self-despair;
> Speak to my heart, in blessings speak,
> Be conquered by my instant prayer.
> Speak, or thou never hence shalt move,
> And tell me if thy name is Love.
>
> 'Tis Love! 'tis Love! Thou died'st for me!
> I hear thy whisper in my heart!
> The morning breaks, the shadows flee;
> Pure universal love thou art;
> To me, to all, thy mercies move;
> Thy nature and thy name is Love.

Night by night, day by day,
let me drink deeper
of that Love,
explore that Nature,
and in that Name find rest.
Amen.

4. Smoke on the mountain

On the morning of the third day there were thunders and lightnings, and a thick cloud upon the mountain, and a very loud trumpet blast, so that all the people who were in the camp trembled. Then Moses brought the people out of the camp to meet God; and they took their stand at the foot of the mountain. And Mount Sinai was wrapped in smoke, because the LORD descended upon it in fire; and the smoke of it went up like the smoke of a kiln, and the whole mountain quaked greatly. And as the sound of the trumpet grew louder and louder, Moses spoke, and God answered him in thunder. And the LORD came down upon Mount Sinai, to the top of the mountain; and the LORD called Moses to the top of the mountain, and Moses went up. And the LORD said to Moses, 'Go down and warn the people, lest they break through to the LORD to gaze and many of them perish. And also let the priests who come near to the LORD consecrate themselves, lest the LORD break out upon them ...'

And God spoke all these words, saying,

'I am the LORD your God, who brought you out of the land of Egypt, out of the house of bondage.

'You shall have no other gods before me.

'You shall not make for yourself a graven image, or any likeness of anything that is in heaven above, or that is in the earth beneath, or that is in the water under the earth; you shall not bow down to them or serve them; for I the LORD your God am a jealous God, visiting the iniquity of the fathers upon the children to the third and the fourth generation of those who hate me, but showing steadfast love to thousands of those who love me and keep my commandments.'

Exodus 19: 16–22; 20: 1–6

What shape is an idol?

I worship Ganesa, brother, god of worldly wisdom, patron of shop-keepers. He is in the shape of a little fat man with an elephant's head; he is made of soapstone and has two small rubies for eyes. What shape do you worship?

I worship a Rolls-Royce sports model, brother. All my days I give it offerings of oil and polish. Hours of my time are devoted to its ritual; and it brings me luck in all my undertakings; and it establishes me among my fellows as a success in life. What model is your car, brother?

I worship my house beautiful, sister. Long and loving meditation have I spent on it; the chairs contrast with the rug, the curtains harmonize with the woodwork, all of it is perfect and holy. The ash trays are in exactly the right place, and should some blasphemer drop ashes on the floor, I nearly die of shock. I live only for the service of my house, and it rewards me with the envy of my sisters, who must rise up and call me blessed. Lest my children profane the holiness of my house with dirt and noise, I drive them out of doors. What shape is your idol, sister? Is it your house, or your clothes, or perhaps even your worth-while and cultural club?

I worship the pictures I paint, brother. . . . I worship my job; I'm the best darn publicity expert this side of Hollywood. . . . I worship my

golf game, my bridge game.... I worship my comfort; after all, isn't
enjoyment the goal of life? ... I worship my church; I want to tell you,
the work we've done in missions beats all other denominations in this
city, and next year we can afford that new organ, and you won't find a
better choir anywhere.... I worship myself....

What shape is *your* idol?

Joy Davidman

Who are you, Lord?
I know the answer:
'I am the Lord your God.'
You are my Father-God,
the God and Father of my Lord
Jesus Christ.
And you are the God of Sinai, too,
who brought Israel from Egypt—
and who brings all your children out of the house of bondage:
You are the Lord my God.

And do I, for whom Sinai is far away,
the smoke on the mountain only distant haze,
do I have other gods? Do I?
Where does liking turn into loving
or serving into worshipping?
What shape is an idol?
Perhaps it is much the shape that I am myself?
For are not all worldly things of value to me
chiefly because they minister to
me?
My pride, my comfort, my keeping-up-with-the-Joneses,
my reputation, popularity, taste, importance,
my gifts, my work, my writing (certainly that)
—even (O God!)
my church, my ministry.

And so I pray for a clearer vision of the God you really are;
a smoking mountain for a modern man.
I pray for such a sense of your
divine holiness, numinous, transcendent,
that 'My' may cease to matter.
Keep me from idols, Lord:
and make me willing to be kept.
For Jesus' glorious Name.
Amen.

5. The weight of years

'See, I have set before you this day life and good, death and evil. If you obey the commandments of the LORD *your God which I command you this day, by loving the* LORD *your God, by walking in his ways, and by keeping his commandments and his statutes and his ordinances, then you shall live and multiply, and the* LORD *your God will bless you in the land which you are entering to take possession of it. But if your heart turns away, and you will not hear, but are drawn away to worship other gods and serve them, I declare to you this day, that you shall perish; you shall not live long in the land which you are going over the Jordan to enter and possess. I call heaven and earth to witness against you this day, that I have set before you life and death, blessing and curse; therefore choose life, that you and your descendants may live, loving the* LORD *your God, obeying his voice, and cleaving to him; for that means life to you and length of days, that you may dwell in the land which the* LORD *swore to your fathers, to Abraham, to Isaac, and to Jacob, to give them.'*

Deuteronomy 30: 15–20

As a sinful man looking at death and beyond it, into the eternal world, I need salvation. Nothing else will meet my case. There is something genuinely at stake in every man's life, the climax whereof is death. Dying is inevitable, but arriving at the destination God offers to me is not inevitable. It is not impossible to go out of the way and fail to arrive. Christian doctrine has always urged that life eternal is something which may conceivably be missed. It is possible to neglect this great salvation and to lose it eternally, even though no man may say that anything is impossible with God or that his grace may ultimately be defeated.

I know it is no longer fashionable to talk about Hell, one good reason for this being that to make religion into a prudential insurance policy is to degrade it. The Faith is not a fire-escape. But in rejecting the old mythology of eternity as grotesque and even immoral, many people make the mistake of rejecting the truth it illustrated (which is rather like rejecting a book as untrue because the pictures in it are bad). It is illogical to tell men that they must do the will of God and accept his gospel of grace, if you also tell them that the obligation has no eternal significance, and that nothing ultimately depends on it. The curious modern heresy that everything is bound to come right in the end is so frivolous that I will not insult you by refuting it. 'I remember', said Dr Johnson on one occasion, 'that my Maker has said that he will place the sheep on his right hand and the goats on his left.' That is a solemn truth which only the empty-headed and empty-hearted will neglect. It strikes at the very roots of life and destiny.

J. S. Whale

O God, I wish,
I wish I were still a child.

Part of the weight of years is this
command to choose:
and you know (who better!) how bad I am at choosing.

I do choose—too often!
I *have* chosen. And I have chosen life, and
claimed your covenant, and set my face to
walk your ways, towards that 'destinatior
which God offers me'.
And then?
THUD
flat on my silly face, miles off-track, enticed
away by some elementary temptation,
the same old world, or flesh, or devil,
and all my choice, and resolution, and commitment—
all to do again.

      And yet not all.
You take my choices, Lord, for what they are.
I could not choose except your Spirit prompted me.
And after that, it is in your salvation, not my
choosing
that hope of heaven rests.

So that in fact, with you, I am a child
—your child, indeed:
wayward, foolish, selfish, disobedient
—and still your child.
Your gospel of grace is my assurance:
and length of days, yes, life eternal
is my inheritance.

Thank you, my Lord.

Amen.

6. The human condition

'Man that is born of a woman is of
few days, and full of trouble.
He comes forth like a flower, and
withers;
he flees like a shadow, and continues not.
And dost thou open thy eyes upon
such a one
and bring him into judgment with
thee?
Who can bring a clean thing out of an
unclean?
There is not one.
Since his days are determined,
and the number of his months is
with thee,
and thou hast appointed his bounds
that he cannot pass,
look away from him, and desist,
that he may enjoy, like a hireling,
his day.
For there is hope for a tree,
if it be cut down, that it will sprout
again,
and that its shoots will not cease.
Though its root grow old in the earth,
and its stump die in the ground,
yet at the scent of water it will bud and
put forth branches like a young
plant.
But man dies, and is laid low;
man breathes his last, and where is
he?
As waters fail from a lake,
and a river wastes away and dries
up,
so man lies down and rises not again;
till the heavens are no more he
will not awake,
or be roused out of his sleep.'

Job 14: 1–12

When all is said, however, the deepest tragedy of life resides, not in those sufferings which seem to fall in such different measures on different men, but in such conditions of earthly existence as are common to us all. The ultimate sadness is that nothing lasts; that the bloom so soon disappears from all things that are young, that the vigour of maturity is so short-lived, while age brings weariness and forgetfulness and decay such as presage the oblivion and corruption of the grave. This is why 'our sincerest laughter with some pain is fraught'. To call to mind the care-free days of youth, to see the friends of youth disappear one by one from our earthly company with hopes only half-fulfilled and work only half done, and to know that no task of our own can ever be completed or any joy held in possession for more than a few fleeting years—this is our great heaviness of heart. And for it I know no healing, nor for the problem of suffering any final prospect of solution, save as we are able to share St Paul's faith when he cries, 'For I reckon that the sufferings of this present time are not worthy to be compared with the glory which shall be revealed in us'.

About our human suffering, therefore, Christianity has ultimately the same thing to say to us as about our human sin—it repeats to us the story of the life and suffering and death and resurrection of Jesus Christ. The solution of both problems is somehow in that story. We there learn of One who spent His life in the relief of the sufferings of others and left His disciples an example that they should follow in His steps. We there learn that in Him 'we have not a high priest which cannot be touched with the feeling of our infirmities; but was in all points tempted like as we are, yet without sin', having 'learned obedience by the things which he suffered'. There we learn also that 'through the obedience of one shall the many be made righteous', that His sufferings were for our sakes and were an instrument of blessing not only to Himself but to the whole sinning and suffering world of men. And there we learn finally that, having suffered and died on our behalf, 'now is Christ risen from the dead, and become the firstfruits of them that slept', and that 'if so be that we suffer with him', it is 'that we may be also glorified together'.

John Baillie

My Father, I thank you with all my heart
that though the human condition
speaks to me of hopes unfulfilled,
of the mark missed,
the bloom fading, the chill of autumn
and beyond that the dark,
yet the Christian condition is
joy.

     'O come let us *sing* unto the Lord,
let us heartily *rejoice* ... and show ourselves *glad* in him ...'

My Father, I am glad in you this morning;
your Name, your Word, your presence
are to me the scent of water. In your hand
no ultimate sadness ultimately holds me.

My Father, I look anew to Jesus.
Let me not lose, in the joy your Spirit gives,
the edge of anguish, the ache of longing,
the waste of spirit like a failing stream,
a river running into sand.
For these I share
with all the family of man. Only,
I find them transformed, resolved, and
turned to hope of glory
within the family of Christ.

My Father, for him, and for knowledge of him,
I thank you, with all my heart.
Amen.

7. Night sky and seashore

O LORD, our Lord,
how majestic is thy name in all the
    earth!

Thou whose glory above the heavens
    is chanted
by the mouth of babes and infants,
thou hast founded a bulwark because
    of thy foes,
    to still the enemy and the avenger.

When I look at thy heavens, the work
    of thy fingers,
    the moon and the stars which thou
    hast established;
    what is man that thou art mindful
    of him,
    and the son of man that thou dost
    care for him?

Yet thou hast made him little less than
    God,
    and dost crown him with glory and
    honour.
Thou hast given him dominion over
    the works of thy hands;
    thou hast put all things under his
    feet,
all sheep and oxen,
    and also the beasts of the field,
the birds of the air, and the fish of the
    sea,
    whatever passes along the paths of
    the sea.

O LORD, our Lord,
    how majestic is thy name in all the
    earth!

Psalm 8

A thought on the seashore

In ev'ry object here I see
Something, O Lord, that leads to thee;
Firm as the rocks thy promise stands,
Thy mercies countless as the sands,
Thy love a sea immensely wide,
Thy grace an ever-flowing tide.

In ev'ry object here I see
Something, my heart, that points at thee:
Hard as the rocks that bound the strand,
Unfruitful as the barren sand,
Deep and deceitful as the ocean,
And, like the tides, in constant motion.

John Newton

O Lord, our Lord—
My Lord too—
When did I last stop for a moment,
alone, in the dark,
really to look at the heavens,
to consider them,
to see them as the work of your hands?
That's another of the many things in this
busy life
that we might all do more often.
   But I have looked: and felt my line of vision
reaching out and out through space,
through light years and incalculable distances,
past the familiar names of unimaginable words—
Pulsars and Red Dwarfs and Black Holes—
words whose very meanings I do not understand.
Out and out and out,
worlds without end.

   The work of your fingers—just as my fingers,
writing these words,
are the work of your fingers too.
The busy mechanism, the cells and tissue,
the nerves and muscles,
the whorled and wrinkled skin,
the sense, the cunning, the quick obedience:
you made us all, our world and all worlds,
O Lord, my Lord.

And what am I, to know
your promises, your mercies, your grace, your love?
Suppose my heart is (as I can only too well believe)
hard, unfruitful, deep, deceitful—
is that beyond the power of
fingers that made the heavens?

O majestic Lord, you care for me,
you have me in your mind and heart.
In that I rest.

Amen.

8. God's world

The fool says in his heart,
'There is no God.'
They are corrupt, they do abominable
deeds,
there is none that does good.

The LORD *looks down from heaven*
upon the children of men,
to see if there are any that act
wisely,
that seek after God.

They have all gone astray, they are all
alike corrupt;
there is none that does good,
no, not one.

Have they no knowledge, all the evil-
doers
who eat up my people as they eat
bread,
and do not call upon the LORD?

There they shall be in great terror,
for God is with the generation of
the righteous.
You would confound the plans of the
poor,
but the LORD *is his refuge.*

O that deliverance for Israel would
come out of Zion!
When the LORD *restores the for-*
tunes of his people.
Jacob shall rejoice, Israel shall be
glad.

Psalm 14

As an explanation of the world, materialism has a sort of insane simplicity. It has just the quality of the madman's argument; we have at once the sense of it covering everything and the sense of it leaving everything out. Contemplate some able and sincere materialist ... and you will have exactly this unique sensation. He understands everything, and everything does not seem worth understanding. His cosmos may be complete in every rivet and cog-wheel, but still his cosmos is smaller than our world. Somehow his scheme, like the lucid scheme of the madman, seems unconscious of the alien energies and the large indifference of the earth; it is not thinking of the real things of the earth, of fighting peoples or proud mothers, or first love or fear upon the sea. The earth is so very large, and the cosmos is so very small. The cosmos is about the smallest hole that a man can hide his head in.

G. K. Chesterton

Open my eyes, O Lord my God;
let me see—really see—
the world I live in.
Let that moment of vision which comes
sometimes
when I least expect it
confirm my knowledge that this,
my home,
is your marvellous and mysterious world.
　　　Help me to see beneath the surface,
to know in heart as well as in mind,
and to have confidence in what
my seeing says.

Part of my trouble is, Lord,
that it's not the fool—or at least
not obviously so—
who says today, 'There is no God.'
The cleverest people,
the most intellectual,
they say it too.
　　　Perhaps it is no accident that the Psalmist
links knowledge with morality—
what a man does
with what he thinks in his heart.
Evildoing comes more easily, he seems to say,
if your heart tells you,
'There is no God.'

So Lord, even while I look beyond it,
help me to attend to the real things of earth—
to read the lessons of experience,
to study the signals,
hinting rather than proclaiming
that this is your world before it is mine.
Help me to live as well as say
'There is a God: he shows himself to men.
In Christ he shows himself to me.'

Amen.

9. Like grass in summer

Lord, thou hast been our dwelling place
in all generations.

Before the mountains were brought forth,
  or ever thou hadst formed the earth and the world,
  from everlasting to everlasting thou art God.

Thou turnest man back to the dust,
  and sayest, 'Turn back, O children of men!'
For a thousand years in thy sight
  are but as yesterday when it is past,
  or as a watch in the night.

Thou dost sweep men away; they are like a dream,
  like grass which is renewed in the morning:

in the morning it flourishes and is renewed;
  in the evening it fades and withers.

For we are consumed by thy anger;
  by thy wrath we are overwhelmed.
Thou hast set our iniquities before thee,
  our secret sins in the light of thy countenance.

For all our days pass away under thy wrath,
  our years come to an end like a sigh.
The years of our life are threescore and ten,
  or even by reason of strength fourscore;
yet their span is but toil and trouble;
  they are soon gone, and we fly away.

Psalm 90: 1–10

The two children

'Ah, little boy! I see
  You have a wooden spade.
Into this sand you dig
  So deep—for what?' I said.
'There's more rich gold', said he,
  'Down under where I stand,
Than twenty elephants
  Could move across the land.'

'Ah, little girl with wool!
  What are you making now?'
'Some stockings for a bird,
  To keep his legs from snow.'
And there those children are,
  So happy, small and proud:
The little boy that digs his grave,
  The girl that knits her shroud.

W. H. Davies

O God,
you are from everlasting
to everlasting.
Time has no place in your being,
as best I can understand it.
You stay the same. You have no
weight of years.

But we are dying now. From the day we are born
we begin to die. And for me,
as I grow older,
time flies so much faster. The world knows it—
'Here today and gone tomorrow,' we say cheerfully—
'Gather ye rosebuds while ye may'!
And sometimes, Lord, I can feel it for myself—
my life melting away like smoke,
fading like a dream,
like grass in summer. My days
'swifter than a weaver's shuttle'.

So:
So let me gather those rosebuds! Make the
most of your good creation.
So let me, as I pass from dust to dust,
use this one life so miraculously given.
So let me find a purpose in serving, caring,
loving.
So let me bring my days, one by one,
into your presence. Day by day, Lord,
be my dwelling place.

Until that day when, my sins forgiven,
my watch below completed,
my work done,
the day breaks and shadows flee away.
For Jesus' sake.

Amen.

10. A foot of ground

O LORD, *thou hast searched me and known me!*
Thou knowest when I sit down and when I rise up;
thou discernest my thoughts from afar.
Thou searchest out my path and my lying down,
and art acquainted with all my ways.
Even before a word is on my tongue,
lo, O LORD, *thou knowest it altogether.*
Thou dost beset me behind and before,
and layest thy hand upon me.
Such knowledge is too wonderful for me;
it is high, I cannot attain it.

Whither shall I go from thy Spirit?
Or whither shall I flee from thy presence?
If I ascend to heaven, thou art there!
If I make my bed in Sheol, thou art there!
If I take the wings of the morning
and dwell in the uttermost parts of the sea,
even there thy hand shall lead me,
and thy right hand shall hold me.
If I say, 'Let only darkness cover me,
and the light about me be night,'
even the darkness is not dark to thee,
the night is bright as the day;
for darkness is as light with thee.

Psalm 139: 1–12

God our refuge

If there had anywhere appeared in space
    Another place of refuge where to flee,
Our hearts had taken refuge from that place,
    And not with Thee.

For we against creation's bars had beat
    Like prisoned eagles, through great worlds had sought
Though but a foot of ground to plant our feet,
    Where Thou wert not.

And only when we found in earth and air,
    In heaven or hell, that such might nowhere be—
That we could not flee from Thee anywhere,
    We fled to Thee.

Richard Chenevix Trench

'Almighty God,
unto whom all hearts be open,
all desires known,
and from whom no secrets are hid . . .'

Almighty, all-seeing God, you have
searched me and known me,
and I confess
that often enough, like Adam,
I have tried to hide in the trees of the garden.
        I have loved darkness rather than light—because
darkness can cover me:
but 'darkness and light are both alike to thee'.
I know that feeling
the poet speaks of:
I too have sought that foot of ground.

Forgive me for the times I hid from,
                        I forgot,
                        I ignored,
                        I turned my back upon
the pleading of your Holy Spirit.

Forgive me that I should have wanted
that dark corner,
that imagined freedom beyond creation's bars,
that place of refuge.
        Forgive, Lord, and understand.
Make me rejoice in your knowledge of me,
not resent it.
Let me be glad that you know me better than I shall
ever know myself.
Teach me to flee to the shadow of
your wings
and there find rest.

Amen.

11. Time and experience

For everything there is a season, and a time for every matter under heaven:
a time to be born, and a time to die;
a time to plant, and a time to pluck up what is planted;
a time to kill, and a time to heal;
a time to break down, and a time to build up;
a time to weep, and a time to laugh;
a time to mourn, and a time to dance;
a time to cast away stones, and a time to gather stones together;
a time to embrace, and a time to refrain from embracing;
a time to seek, and a time to lose;
a time to keep, and a time to cast away;
a time to rend, and a time to sew;
a time to keep silence, and a time to speak;
a time to love, and a time to hate;
a time for war, and a time for peace.
What gain has the worker from his toil?

I have seen the business that God has given to the sons of men to be busy with. He has made everything beautiful in its time; also he has put eternity into man's mind, yet so that he cannot find out what God has done from the beginning to the end. I know that there is nothing better for them than to be happy and enjoy themselves as long as they live; also that it is God's gift to man that every one should eat and drink and take pleasure in all his toil. I know that whatever God does endures for ever; nothing can be added to it, nor anything taken from it; God has made it so, in order that men should fear before him.

Ecclesiastes 3: 1–14

It is one of the more unjustifiable pretensions of our age that it measures time and experience by the clock. There are obviously a host of considerations and values which a clock cannot possibly measure. There is, above all, the fact that time spent on a journey, particularly on a journey which sets in motion the abiding symbolism of our natures, is different from the time devoured at such a terrifying speed in the daily routine of what is accepted, with such curious complacency, as our normal lives. This seems axiomatic to me; the truer the moment and the greater its content of reality the slower the swing of the universal pendulum.

Let me give an instance. I could imagine a moment denied to a life as soiled as my own—a moment so real that time would come to a standstill within it, would cease to exist despite all the ticking of clocks that went on. I do not want to claim too much for this humble, this unwinged moment there on the aerodrome at Nairobi. But I must emphasize, as best I can in dealing with a reaction that is beyond the normal use of words, that there was more to it than a mere twenty-four hours measured on the clock. Somehow the barriers between all of us had been down, the masks over our eyes had been lifted and we had become genuinely and unusually well-disposed to one another.

Laurens Van der Post

Who knows the workings of a human heart?
    You do, my Father, my creator God.
Who knows the mystery of heavenly
echoes and spiritual desire?
    You know, my Father; you put them there.
Who knows what it feels like to be truly human?
    You know, Lord Jesus, Son of Man.

And I know too.
At least, I know something
—perhaps a very little. But under
the torrent of conflicting voices, the
rushing busyness of life,
I catch momentarily (sometimes when
I least expect it) the lifting of a curtain
on an eternal world which is yet
home.

    And so my prayer is this:
that I may know ever more clearly
that these moments of perception
speak of a real world—indeed, in the end the only
real world.
Help me to attend, to welcome
the Spirit's voice within; to sit
more loosely
to the ticking clocks that measure only
natural time.
You gave me, Lord,
a nature
not contained in Nature,
a toehold in eternity.
Help me to live this life
better, more fully, more up to my full
capacities
because it is your good world,
but not your eternal world,
my changeless Lord.
Amen.

12. Youth and age

Remember also your Creator in the days of your youth, before the evil days come, and the years draw nigh, when you will say, 'I have no pleasure in them'; before the sun and the light and the moon and the stars are darkened and the clouds return after the rain; in the day when the keepers of the house tremble, and the strong men are bent, and the grinders cease because they are few, and those that look through the windows are dimmed, and the doors on the street are shut; when the sound of the grinding is low, and one rises up at the voice of a bird, and all the daughters of sons are brought low; they are afraid also of what is high, and terrors are in the way; the almond tree blossoms, the grass-hopper drags itself along and desire fails; because man goes to his eternal home, and the mourners go about the streets; before the silver cord is snapped, or the golden bowl is broken, or the pitcher is broken at the fountain, or the wheel broken at the cistern, and the dust returns to the earth as it was, and the spirit returns to God who gave it. Vanity of vanities, says the Preacher; all is vanity.

Ecclesiastes 12: 1–8

There is the chill of winter in the air of verse 2, as the rains persist and the clouds turn daylight into gloom, and then night into pitch blackness. It is a scene sombre enough to bring home to us not only the fading of physical and mental powers but the more general desolations of old age. There are many lights that are liable then to be withdrawn, besides those of the senses and faculties, as, one by one, old friends are taken, familiar customs change, and long-held hopes now have to be abandoned. All this will come at a stage when there is no longer the resilience of youth or the prospect of recovery to offset it. In one's early years, and for the greater part of life, troubles and illnesses are chiefly set-backs, not disasters. One expects the sky to clear eventually. It is hard to adjust to the closing of that long chapter: to know that now, in the final stretch, there will be no improvement: the clouds will always gather again, and time will no longer heal, but kill.

So it is in youth, not age, that these inexorable facts are best confronted, when they can drive us into action—that total response to God which was the subject of verse 1—not into despair and vain regrets.

In verses 3 and 4a the picture changes. Now it is no longer one of nightfall, storm and winter, but of a great house in decline. Its former glories of power, style, liveliness and hospitality can now be surmised only by contrast with their few, pathetic relics. In the brave struggle to survive there is almost a more pointed reminder of decay than in a total ruin. It is still part of our own scene; our own future is facing us and we cannot avoid involvement with this foretaste of it.

That picture, to my mind, is best taken in its entirety, not laboriously broken down into the constituent metaphors for human arms, legs, teeth, and so on, which doubtless underlie it—as though the poet had expressed himself inadequately. The dying house reveals us to ourselves as no mere catalogue or inventory could.

Derek Kidner

Lord, you made me: you
and no other are
my Creator. And in your sight
all the mysterious processes of mind
and spirit—unconscious depths and
unrecognized desires—lie plain as day.
    And now, on this journey
—common to all of us—from
youth to age, I do remember you,
and when I start to count your blessings to me,
like sheep in a gateway, I see no end.
    I look round at today's life, Lord:
busy, preoccupied, varied,
rich in stresses and rhythms of work
and rest and change. Now, Lord, in
the rush of life, pressed by the cares of the world,
getting and spending, too few hours in the day,
let me find time, Lord, to remember you.
    And what of the future?
My times are in your hand: and I would not
change that, Lord. But I forsee
new experiences ahead. Time will come
to lay things down; to cease to plan ahead;
to find the lights going out,
the scene contracting; work, for good or ill,
done or undone, beyond my powers.
Lord, against that time, I remember you.
    Let me learn, now, to trust myself
to your safe keeping
as once I learned, splashing and struggling,
to trust myself to swim. Let me be ready,
unresisting, in calm and peace and joy,
to float upon your tide.

So make me ready now against that day.

Amen.

13. Text for a great sinner

Hear the word of the LORD,
you rulers of Sodom!
Give ear to the teaching of our God,
you people of Gomorrah!
'What to me is the multitude of your
sacrifices?
says the LORD;
I have had enough of burnt offerings
of rams
and the fat of fed beasts;
I do not delight in the blood of bulls,
or of lambs, or of he-goats.

Your new moons and your appointed
feasts
my soul hates;
they have become a burden to me,
I am weary of bearing them.
When you spread forth your hands,
I will hide my eyes from you;
even though you make many prayers,
I will not listen;
your hands are full of blood.

Wash yourselves; make yourselves
clean;
remove the evil of your doings
from before my eyes;
cease to do evil,
learn to do good;
seek justice,
correct oppression;
defend the fatherless,
plead for the widow.

'Come now, let us reason together,
says the LORD:
though your sins are like scarlet,
they shall be as white as snow;
though they are red like crimson,
they shall become like wool.
If you are willing and obedient,
you shall eat the good of the land;
But if you refuse and rebel,
you shall be devoured by the
sword;
for the mouth of the LORD *has*
spoken.'

Isaiah 1: 10, 11, 14–20

Mrs Christopher was an invalid for two years, and upon her death in 1836—she was the first of the family to be buried in the Christopher vault in Chiswick churchyard—Isabella nevertheless believed she had not done all she might for her, and fell into a state of morbid despair. 'She was the most holy one of the family,' Alfred wrote in after years, 'in the eyes of her brothers and sisters, yet she thought she could not be saved. I was her young brother of 16 years of age, who knew but little of the Bible. I had only one qualification for helping her, which was this: I felt certain that if anything could help her, it must be in the Bible, for she would care for no book of less authority. So I began to search the Scriptures. I thought there was a great probability of finding something that would help to comfort and encourage her in "the Book of the Prophet Isaiah." So I began to read the first Chapter of that Book. When I came to the 18th verse, 'Come now, and let us reason together, saith the Lord: though your sins be as scarlet, they shall be as white as snow; though they be red like crimson they shall be as wool,' I started up and ran upstairs to my dear sister's bedside. I felt that was a text suited for a great sinner, which was what my dear sister thought herself to be, though all her family knew her to be a great saint. I repeated this one verse over and over again. My most effective sermon

40

was all text & *nothing in addition* to it. In her 95th year I asked her 'What was the text which restored you, through the Spirit Who used it, to peace, health and usefulness?' She repeated Isaiah 1: 18. She said "That text was *thumped* into my heart all night as I lay awake." I had forgotten the text, but I think I never can forget my sister's answer to my question.'

J. S. Reynolds

What if your door, my God, is shut against me?
What if I spread forth my hands,
and make my prayers—
only to know your eyes are averted,
your attention is elsewhere,
you will not listen?
O God, what then?

Who was it—Esau?—who
found no place of repentance
'though he sought it with tears'?
Isabella sought like that. Israel
should have done so. And I? How lightly
sometimes I accept forgiveness.
So let me look, holding my Father's hand
as a child looks over a cliff
to measure again
something of what sin is,
and of God's promises to fallen man.
My sins are not scarlet, for the most part,
—just dirty discoloured stains. They too
can be white as snow.

O God my Father, O Lamb of God,
my Saviour.
Keep me in repentance as well as faith.
Help me to work away at obedience and righteousness.
Let me spread forth my hands
and know you hear me; confess my sins
and know forgiveness;
cease to do evil, learn to do good.
Through Jesus Christ, my Lord.
Amen.

14. A vision of reality

In the year that King Uzziah died I saw the Lord sitting upon a throne, high and lifted up; and his train filled the temple. Above him stood the seraphim; each had six wings; with two he covered his face, and with two he covered his feet, and with two he flew. And one called to another and said:

'Holy, holy, holy is the LORD *of hosts;*

the whole earth is full of his glory.'
And the foundations of the thresholds shook at the voice of him who called, and the house was filled with smoke. And I said: 'Woe is me! For I am lost; for I am a man of unclean lips, and I dwell in the midst of a people of unclean lips; for my eyes have seen the King, the LORD *of hosts!'*

Then flew one of the seraphim to me, having in his hand a burning coal which he had taken with tongs from the altar. And he touched my mouth, and said: 'Behold, this has touched your lips; your guilt is taken away, and your sin forgiven.' And I heard the voice of the Lord saying, 'Whom shall I send, and who will go for us?' Then I said, 'Here am I! Send me.' And he said, 'Go, and say to this people:*

'Hear and hear, but do not understand;

see and see, but do not perceive.'
Make the heart of this people fat,
and their ears heavy,
and shut their eyes;
lest they see with their eyes,
and hear with their ears,
and understand with their hearts,
and turn and be healed.'' '
Then I said, 'How long, O Lord?'

Isaiah 6: 1–11

It is so difficult for theologians to survive all the experiences which would qualify them to write. They must have seen a vision of reality, without which all the rest is cheap; they must have been through the modern disciplines of history and science, so that they can think in those languages and come to terms with their findings; they must have read all the previous theology, and then forgotten it, which is the test most theologians are unable to pass; they must have the poetry of life in their veins. And when they have all, or most of these, too often they are cramped by language now grown familiar, and by love of something which has once meant truth. . . .

What we are waiting for from the theologians is a restatement of the Drama of Salvation in a form convincing to this generation. Sin, salvation and the Kingdom of God are as real as ever they were. Direct experience should produce direct expression. But there are psychologists who can speak more directly to the age than some theologians can, and who appear to understand the soul of man better. These psychologists may be unable within their own self-limited field to take the next and needed step; indeed they may not have the experience. So they too fail us. It is the combination of the understanding of man's inner life, with the profound experience of the Christian conviction, reinforced by the gift of inspired speech, which we lack.

When John Bunyan produced *Pilgrim's Progress*, these three conditions were fulfilled, and one of the greatest works of Christian theology resulted. It is true that it is not in academic shape, that it is rich in homely speech, that there may be portions which are dated now, that he approaches from the side of man's pilgrimage to the impact of Christ upon his life, that the drama of salvation is actually dramatised. It is the more real for all this.

It is noteworthy that those who have most deeply appropriated the truths of religion can usually, like Bunyan, speak most simply and directly in the language of those they are addressing.

G. L. Heawood

Teach me, my Father, through Isaiah's vision.
Let me see, upon that inward eye,
the throne, the temple, the seraphim,
the Lord
and with this vision, let me also see
behind the scaffolding of human language
to the knowledge of God.

I know, my Father, that the nearer I come,
the more I share Isaiah's self-knowledge—
'Woe is me, woe is me'.
Still let me come: until I hear like him
the Lord's voice—your voice, my Father—
saying, 'Whom shall I send?'

How can I answer you, Lord?
If I say 'Send me', then
who am I?
What first-hand vision have I to share?

Yet how can I not say 'Send me'?
My generation needs to hear.
The fire still burns: so touch me
—tongue and mouth and heart and mind—
from the secret places of the Spirit's glow.
Open my eyes to a new vision of your holiness;
open my mind and understanding;
open my mouth to be your messenger;
O Lord of Hosts,
O God my Father,
here am I: send me.
Amen.

15. Prisoners and captives

The Spirit of the Lord GOD *is upon me,*
because the LORD *has anointed me*
to bring good tidings to the afflicted;
he has sent me to bind up the brokenhearted,
to proclaim liberty to the captives,
and the opening of the prison
to those who are bound;
to proclaim the year of the LORD'S *favour,*
and the day of vengeance of our God;
to comfort all who mourn;
to grant to those who mourn in Zion—
to give them a garland instead of ashes,
the oil of gladness instead of mourning,
the mantle of praise instead of a faint spirit;
that they may be called oaks of righteousness,
the planting of the LORD, *that he may be glorified.*

They shall build up the ancient ruins,
they shall raise up the former devastations;
they shall repair the ruined cities,
the devastations of many generations. . . .
I will greatly rejoice in the LORD,
my soul shall exult in my God;
for he has clothed me with the garments of salvation,
he has covered me with the robe of righteousness,
as a bridegroom decks himself with a garland,
and as a bride adorns herself with her jewels.
For as the earth brings forth its shoots,
and as a garden causes what is sown in it to spring up,
so the Lord GOD *will cause righteousness and praise*
to spring forth before all the nations.

Isaiah 61: 1–4; 10, 11

Tiny was another man who had been converted in jail and who came out and worked with the Narcotics Committee. He was a big jovial Negro with a happy-go-lucky air and a great gift for friendship with those who sought help from the Parish. One cold March night, when he had been off drugs for a year and a half, he was to receive the Commendation Card which was given every quarter to those who had successfully abstained. Norm Eddy picked up Tiny's card from the office table, and glanced round the circle of addicts and narcotics workers, before he said, 'On your behalf, I want to give this Commendation Card to our committeeman, Tiny Scott.' A chair scraped as Tiny rose to his feet. He hesitated uncertainly, then muttered as he made his way to the door, 'I don't want to accept till I get a few things straightened out. . . .' And the door let in a cold blast of air before it closed again behind him. Tiny had gone back on heroin. And those who had worked and worshipped with him, whose lives were intertwined with his, never saw him in the office again. All they heard of him was what he wrote after fighting for three long weeks to keep of heroin: when he lost yet one more fight, and the after-effects of the drug had left him utterly dejected, he wrote his terrible 'psalm' and pushed it under Pee-Wee's door:

Heroin is my shepherd
I shall always want
It maketh me to lie down in gutters
It leadeth me beside still madness
It destroyeth my soul
It leadeth me in the paths of Hell for its name's sake
Yea, though I walk through the Valley of the Shadow of Death
I will fear no evil
For heroin art with me
My syringe and spike shall comfort me
Thou puttest me to shame in the presence of mine enemies
Thou anointest my head with madness
My cup runneth over with sorrow
Surely hate and evil shall follow me all the days of my life
And I will dwell in the house of misery and disgrace for ever.

Bruce Kenrick

O Lord God, living God, you have called
your children of the new covenant,
as you called your prophets, to speak your Name
and do your will before the waiting world: to make known
your gospel, to portray your care,
to bind up the brokenhearted, to comfort mourners,
and proclaim release to prisoners and captives.

In what captivities, O Lord, we find our bonds!

And so I pray for all—not least myself—
who know the power of sin to bind and hold:
for all who are fast bound in habits, forms, traditions, rules;
for those who are the slaves of circumstances,
the recurrent victims of besetting sins,
or who have lost their freedom to
companions, masters, vices, follies, lusts.
        I pray for those who see no other prospect
but the house of misery and disgrace for ever.

Lord, may your Spirit's power break in upon them!
May your good news be news to those who need it.
May the ancient ruins, the devastation,
of broken lives and broken hearts
be built anew into a holy temple, a place of freedom,
of praise and righteousness, in Jesus' Name. Amen.

16. Destiny's pattern

'Thus says the LORD *of hosts, the God of Israel, to all the exiles whom I have sent into exile from Jerusalem to Babylon: Build houses and live in them; plant gardens and eat their produce. Take wives and have sons and daughters; take wives for your sons, and give your daughters in marriage, that they may bear sons and daughters; multiply there, and do not decrease. But seek the welfare of the city where I have sent you into exile, and pray to the* LORD *on its behalf, for in its welfare you will find your welfare. For thus says the* LORD *of hosts, the God of Israel: Do not let your prophets and your diviners who are among you deceive you, and do not listen to the dreams which they dream, for it is a lie which they are prophesying to you in my name; I did not send them, says the* LORD.

'For thus says the LORD: *When seventy years are completed for Babylon, I will visit you, and I will fulfil to you my promise and bring you back to this place. For I know the plans I have for you, says the* LORD, *plans for welfare and not for evil, to give you a future and a hope. Then you will call upon me and come and pray to me, and I will hear you. You will seek me and find me; when you seek me with all your heart, I will be found by you, says the* LORD, *and I will restore your fortunes and gather you from all the nations and all the places where I have driven you, says the* LORD, *and I will bring you back to the place from which I sent you into exile.'*

Jeremiah 29: 4–14

One can speak, and truly enough, about pure coincidence, but the Christian may see it from another angle. Looking back on the changing scenes of life, [Mervyn Haigh] was keenly and thankfully aware of an overruling, Providential guidance leading him on from one step to another. In that light he regarded ... all the manifold events which happened so when they might have happened otherwise, starting from the engagement of his parents. In his closing years, with immense labour and difficulty, he put together, partly from memory, partly from documented research, a record of his personal history down to his consecration to Coventry, by way of bearing a Christian witness to it. To that record he gave the title *Opening Doors*. For, as most of us, probably, can see in retrospect, it is frequently by the closing of a door through which we had hoped and planned to go and the unexpected opening of another, that the guiding Hand has been revealed. He tells how he was gradually led through his doubts and misgivings about ordination, through friends he met, through teachers who influenced him, through the lessons of deeply pondered experience, and through the pressure of what we men call 'circumstances' on the path which God intended him to go. The completing of this considerable manuscript laid a heavy strain on his physical resources, and though it gave him great satisfaction, the writing often left him entirely exhausted. He prefaced it with a quotation from the final chapter in Charles Smyth's classic biography of Cyril Garbett: 'It is a commonplace of religious experience that when a Christian looks back over his own individual life—his secular career as well as his spiritual development—it becomes apparent to him that there has been a mysterious pattern running through it all, and that, not by his own initiative, and not always by his own volition, his life has been brought into conformity with that pattern by the hand of God. The evidence for this doctrine of particular Providence in human lives is far too strong to be neglected or ignored.'

F. R. Barry

Lord of my life,
how many things have happened to me
that might have happened otherwise!
Looking back, upon what slender threads
your pattern for me hung! What
insignificant weights
tilted the scale from this to that!
And from this multitude of tiny choices,
unrelated circumstances,
unnoticed influences,
you wove the pattern of my present life!

And all this that I recall, only
the tip of the iceberg! What of the unseen
providences? What of the choices before
I was born or thought of? I join,
Lord, with the children in their
song of praise:
'Thank you, Father, for making me me.'

And if this is true of my past life,
shaped, subtly and beyond imagining, by
the finger of God—
why, I rest my future on your promise too.
You know your plans, Lord, as you did
for Israel in exile. Knowing that
the plans are yours, I do not need
to know much else about them.
Except this: that all you do is good.
So let me seek you, Lord,
your face, your Word, your presence
and your will,
with all my heart.
Amen.

17. Stern love

'At that time, says the LORD, I will be the God of all the families of Israel, and they shall be my people.'
Thus says the LORD:
'The people who survived the sword found grace in the wilderness;
when Israel sought for rest,
the LORD appeared to him from afar.
I have loved you with an everlasting love;
therefore I have continued my faithfulness to you.
Again I will build you, and you shall be built.
O virgin Israel!
Again you shall adorn yourself with timbrels,
and shall go forth in the dance of the merrymakers.
Again you shall plant vineyards upon the mountains of Samaria;
the planters shall plant, and shall enjoy the fruit.
For there shall be a day when watchmen will call
in the hill country of Ephraim:

'Arise, and let us go up to Zion, to the LORD our God." '

For thus says the LORD:
'Sing aloud with gladness for Jacob, and raise shouts for the chief of the nations;
proclaim, give praise, and say,
"The LORD has saved his people, the remnant of Israel."
Behold, I will bring them from the north country,
and gather them from the farthest parts of the earth,
among them the blind and the lame, the woman with child and her who is in travail, together;
a great company, they shall return here.
With weeping they shall come,
and with consolations I will lead them back,
I will make them walk by brooks of water,
in a straight path in which they shall not stumble;
for I am a father to Israel,
and Ephraim is my first-born.'

Jeremiah 31: 1–9

The story of Finchden Manor is overwhelmingly one of happy endings, or rather of happy beginnings, since there the boys were given that chance to start again which life so seldom affords in later years. One thinks of all those other boys, who never went to Finchden, and are now in prison or needlessly unhappy. Over and over again I read in the newspapers the childhood story of some adolescent who was evidently beginning a life of crime; and the details read exactly like the story of some boy who had gone to Finchden, and there been saved, and found himself. . . .

Finchden shows the strength of a treatment rooted in life, and demonstrates the might of disinterested love. Mr Lyward had recreated a lost family, welcoming into it boys whose roots were shrivelled by striking them afresh, and nourishing their natural growth. He disowned none, and never withdrew needed help when the boys had become men. This recreated family, although never able to equal the warmth and strength of the natural family, has none the less illumined the way of love for many parents, and may illumine it for many others, whose love is in danger of becoming parched or distorted by tiredness, possessiveness, or self-interest. . . .

David Norris arrived at Finchden, having been found in possession of a cosh.

'What do you most want?' Mr Lyward asked him.

'A home,' said the boy. 'And I'd have had one if my mum hadn't gone off with the bloody lodger.'

'What would you think of a place where you would be given stern love?' Mr Lyward asked.

'I've never heard of that kind,' the boy answered. 'Sounds as if it might be all right.'

Michael Burns

O Lord God of Israel, your chosen people—
and my God too:
Father to Israel—and Father to me:
I have at moments shared the warmth and faced the demands
of that stern, gentle, everlasting love.
And I know too, my Father,
how often—perhaps always—I would settle for less.

Oh, I want to be your child,
with all that means of family privilege.
But you are a Father not lightly satisfied.
No child of yours can go his own sweet way.
So touch my will,
that I shall not want less than you want, Father, in me, your child.

Your love is never parched, distorted, possessive,
never for your sake, always for mine.
But it is a stern love, a consuming fire,
from which I shrink indeed.
Could not I have, perhaps, a little less?
Your gaze be less intense,
Your standards more relaxed,
Your care more casual?
O God, help me by word and deed
never to pray that prayer!

My Father, in a love-starved world,
let your love have its way in me.
And let my love catch a spark in turn. Amen.

49

18. The Christian difference

Then, at break of day, the king arose and went in haste to the den of lions. When he came near to the den where Daniel was, he cried out in a tone of anguish and said to Daniel, 'O Daniel, servant of the living God, has your God, whom you serve continually, been able to deliver you from the lions?' Then Daniel said to the king, 'O king, live for ever! My God sent his angel and shut the lions' mouths, and they have not hurt me, because I was found blameless before him; and also before you, O king, I have done no wrong.' Then the king was exceedingly glad, and commanded that Daniel be taken up out of the den. So Daniel was taken up out of the den, and no kind of hurt was found upon him, because he had trusted in his God. And the king commanded, and those men who had accused Daniel were brought and cast into the den of lions—they, their children, and their wives; and before they reached the bottom of the den the lions overpowered them and broke all their bones in pieces.

Then King Darius wrote to all the peoples, nations, and languages that dwell in all the earth: 'Peace be multiplied to you. I make a decree, that in all my royal dominion men tremble and fear before the God of Daniel,
for he is the living God,
enduring for ever;
his kingdom shall never be destroyed,
and his dominion shall be to the end.
He delivers and rescues,
he works signs and wonders
in heaven and on earth,
he who has saved Daniel
from the power of the lions.'
So this Daniel prospered during the reign of Darius and the reign of Cyrus the Persian.

Daniel 6: 19–28

There was a young Kikuyu by the name of Kitau, who came in from the Kikuyu Reserve and took service with me. He was a meditative boy, an observant, attentive servant, and I liked him well. After three months he one day asked me to give him a letter of recommendation to my old friend Sheik Ali bin Salim, the *Lewali* of the Coast, at Mombasa, for he had seen him in my house and now, he said, he wished to go and work for him. I did not want Kitau to leave just when he had learned the routine of the house, and I said to him that I would rather raise his pay. No, he said, he was not leaving to get any higher pay, but he could not stay. He told me that he had made up his mind, up in the Reserve, that he would become either a Christian or a Mohammedan, only he did not yet know which. For this reason he had come and worked for me, since I was a Christian, and he had stayed for three months in my house to see the *testurde*—the ways and habits—of the Christians. From me he would go for three months to Sheik Ali in Mombasa and study the *testurde* of the Mohammedans; then he would decide. I believe that even an archbishop, when he had had these facts laid before him, would have said, or at least have thought, as I said: 'Good God, Kitau, you might have told me that when you came here.'

Karen Blixen

50

O God, the living God,
enduring for ever,
who saved Daniel from the power of the lions,
who delivers and rescues,
who works signs and wonders in heaven and earth—
O God, my God,
what about me?

I know and trust in your deliverance,
your rescuing,
your Kingdom,
your power and your glory, for ever and ever, Amen;
but where is your power today?
Where is your present glory
to be seen in me?

     I too have friends who watch me closely,
reassured, I sometimes think,
to see how little different
my standards appear from theirs.
     There is not much—is there, Lord?—
to make men tremble and fear,
or to make others love and worship,
before what can be seen
of God in me.
But you are the living God:
the same today as yesterday.
What you did for Daniel in that
royal court and in that den of lions,
you can do for me in my
workaday world.

     And so I dare to pray that,
all unknown to us who serve you,
a Christian difference may yet been seen.
Whoever plays the part of Kitau in my life—
Lord, speak to him.
For Jesus' sake.
Amen.

19. The ground of prayer

Then I turned my face to the Lord God, seeking him by prayer and supplications with fasting and sackcloth and ashes. I prayed to the LORD *my God and made confession, saying ,'O Lord, the great and terrible God, who keepest covenant and steadfast love with those who love him and keep his commandments, we have sinned and done wrong and acted wickedly and rebelled, turning aside from thy commandments and ordinances; we have not listened to thy servants the prophets, who spoke in thy name to our kings, our princes, and our fathers, and to all the people of the land. To thee, O Lord, belongs righteousness, but to us confusion of face, as at this day, to the men of Judah, to the inhabitants of Jerusalem, and to all Israel, those that are near and those that are far away, in all the lands to which thou has driven them, because of the treachery which they have committed against thee. . . . Now therefore, O our God, hearken to the prayer of thy servant and to his supplications, and for thy own sake, O Lord, cause thy face to shine upon thy sanctuary, which is desolate. O my God, incline thy ear and hear; open thy eyes and behold our desolations, and the city which is called by thy name; for we do not present our supplications before thee on the ground of our righteousness, but on the ground of thy great mercy. O* LORD, *hear; O* LORD, *forgive; O* LORD, *give heed and act; delay not, for thy own sake, O my God, because thy city and thy people are called by thy name.'*

While I was speaking and praying, confessing my sin and the sin of my people Israel, and presenting my supplication before the LORD *my God for the holy hill of my God; while I was speaking in prayer, the man Gabriel, whom I had seen in the vision at the first, came to me in swift flight at the time of the evening sacrifice. He came and he said to me, 'O Daniel, I have now come out to give you wisdom and understanding. At the beginning of your supplications a word went forth, and I have come to tell it to you, for you are greatly beloved.'*

Daniel 9: 3–7, 17–23

Our Lord's will

For this is our Lord's will—that our prayer and our trust be alike, large. For if we do not trust as much as we pray, we fail in full worship to our Lord in our prayer; and also we hinder and hurt ourselves. The reason is that we do not know truly that our Lord is the ground from whom our prayer springeth; nor do we know that it is given us by his grace and his love. If we knew this, it would make us trust to have of our Lord's gift all that we desire. For I am sure that no man asketh mercy and grace with sincerity, without mercy and grace being given to him first.

Sometimes it cometh to our mind that we have prayed long time, and yet, seemingly, we have not received an answer. We should not be grieved on this account, but—and I am sure of this in our Lord's meaning—we merely await a better time, a greater grace, or a better gift. He willeth us to have true knowing in him—that he is all-being. In this knowing he willeth that our understanding be grounded, with all our power and all our intent and all our meaning. In this ground he willeth that we take up our station and our dwelling.

The Lady Julian

I turn my face to yours,
O God my Father. The same
'great and terrible God, who keepest
covenant and steadfast love',
the God and Father of Jesus Christ, my Lord.
I turn my face to yours.
　　　　And I can only turn to you, my Father,
because mercy and forgiveness are yours,
because I am called by your Name,
because all your children are greatly beloved.
My Saviour Christ is the ground of my prayer,
your revelation in him the ground of my understanding,
your mercy the ground on which I stand.
　　　　Enlarge my prayer, Lord. Help me to seek patiently
a greater grace,
a better gift,
by using better the grace and gift I have.
Tame my rebellions,
increase my wisdom and understanding.
Fill my poor prayers with all the power, intent and meaning
that they can bear.
　　　　And so enlarge them. Give me a clearer vision
as I turn my face to yours.

And when I turn in shame and confession,
in confusion of face and
desolation of heart,
O Lord, hear:
O Lord, forgive;
O Lord delay not,
for you are the ground of all my praying
and the answer to my prayer.
O Lord, I turn my face to yours
in love.

Amen.

20. To bear his cross

Seeing the crowds, he went up on the mountain, and when he sat down his disciples came to him. And he opened his mouth and taught them, saying:

'Blessed are the poor in spirit, for theirs is the kingdom of heaven.

'Blessed are those who mourn, for they shall be comforted.

'Blessed are the meek, for they shall inherit the earth.

'Blessed are those who hunger and thirst for righteousness, for they shall be satisfied.

'Blessed are the merciful, for they shall obtain mercy.

'Blessed are the pure in heart, for they shall see God.

'Blessed are the peacemakers, for they shall be called sons of God.

'Blessed are those who are persecuted for righteousness' sake, for theirs is the kingdom of heaven.

'Blessed are you when men revile you and persecute you and utter all kinds of evil against you falsely on my account. Rejoice and be glad, for your reward is great in heaven, for so men persecuted the prophets who were before you.'

Matthew 5: 1–12

Charles Simeon in Cambridge

Quite as hard to bear as open insults and attempts at outrage were the coldness and half-exposed contempt of men of his own standing. Indeed this must have been to him the heavier burthen of the two. The disorderly gownsmen challenged and called out his personal courage as well as his patience; the slow trials of social estrangement, surely one of the severest tests of principle to a man of refinement and sensibility, could not be met by action. 'I remember the time that I was quite surprised that a Fellow of my own College ventured to walk with me for a quarter of an hour on the grass-plot before Clare Hall; and for many years after I began my ministry I was "as a man wondered at," by reason of the paucity of those who showed any regard for true religion.'

He records one incident of the inner history of those trying years: 'When I was an object of much contempt and derision in the University, I strolled forth one day, buffeted and afflicted, with my little Testament in my hand. I prayed earnestly to my God that He would comfort me with some cordial from His Word, and that, on opening the book, I might find some text which should sustain me. It was not for direction I was looking, for I am no friend to such superstitions as the *sortes Virgilianae*, but only for support. The first text which caught my eye was this: *"They found a man of Cyrene, Simon by name; him they compelled to bear His cross."* You know Simon is the same name as Simeon. What a word of instruction was here—what a blessed hint for my encouragement! to have the cross laid upon me, that I might bear it after Jesus—what a privilege! It was enough. Now I could leap and sing for joy as one whom Jesus was honouring with a participation of His sufferings.'

H. C. G. Moule

Jesus, my Lord,
you knew so much of insult and reproach,
I know so little, and what I know, I fear.

Where are the people who would not be seen
in my company? And what of that
'contempt and derision' which Simeon knew—
like so many of your servants (like them
all perhaps?) of which I barely know
the taste at all? 'The slow trials
of social estrangement'? Yes, I know something of them.
But probably for what I am,
rather than for what Christ is in me.

Teach me the blessedness of which you spoke:
happiness in humility, emptiness, hunger.
Teach me, as I can bear it, the blessedness of
reproach, scorn, the cold shoulder; but only for your sake.
Deliver me from self-pity,
mock heroics,
dramatizing my poor self.
But 'to have the Cross laid upon me,
that I might bear it after Jesus'—prepare me for
that day, if it should come:
that all the faint forerunners of it may be blessed,
and that it be to me
a day of joy.

Amen.

21. Lord, help me

And Jesus went away from there and withdrew to the district of Tyre and Sidon. And behold, a Canaanite woman from that region came out and cried, 'Have mercy on me, O Lord, Son of David; my daughter is severely possessed by a demon.' But he did not answer her a word. And his disciples came and begged him, saying, 'Send her away, for she is crying after us.' He answered, 'I was sent only to the lost sheep of the house of Israel.' But she came and knelt before him, saying, 'Lord, help me.' And he answered, 'It is not fair to take the children's bread and throw it to the dogs.' She said, 'Yes, Lord, yet even the dogs eat the crumbs that fall from their master's table.' Then Jesus answered her, 'O woman, great is your faith! Be it done for you as you desire.' And her daughter was healed instantly.

And Jesus went on from there and passed along the Sea of Galilee. And he went up into the hills, and sat down there. And great crowds came to him, bringing with them the lame, the maimed, the blind, the dumb, and many others, and they put them at his feet, and he healed them, so that the throng wondered, when they saw the dumb speaking, the maimed whole, the lame walking, and the blind seeing; and they glorified the God of Israel.

Matthew 15: 21–31

A prayer for healing

Here, Master, in this quiet place,
Where anyone may kneel,
I also come to ask for grace,
Believing you can heal.

If pain of body, stress of mind,
Destroys my inward peace,
In prayer for others may I find
The secret of release.

If self upon its sickness feeds,
And turns my life to gall,
Let me not brood upon my needs,
But simply tell you all.

You never said, 'You ask too much'
To any troubled soul.
I long to feel your healing touch—
Will you not make me whole?

But if the thing I most desire
Is not your way for me,
May faith, when tested in the fire,
Prove its integrity.

Of all my prayers, let this be chief:
Till faith is fully grown,
Lord, disbelieve my unbelief,
And claim me as your own.

F. Pratt Green

My Father,
there is so much I would have
different—and which I believe
you would have different too. I want
to make a start. I think it must
begin in me. But where?
  Lord, help me.

And there are others—like this poor woman's daughter—
whom I would bring to you as she brought
this great, this overwhelming need.
There are friends and neighbours I feel
so powerless to help. People I love,
dangerously near the rocks, far from their
true home, possessed by many demons of
our modern world. How can I help them?
How can I serve them better?
  Lord, help me.

And my own deep places—the
unremembered scars which limit me today;
the unhealed wounds that make me less than whole—
  Lord, help me.

My faith is not great, Lord. Indeed
I do not always want true healing.
There are attractions in a certain
undemanding invalidism. But I want
what you want. I trust you where I do not trust myself.

So be my bread of life, Lord Jesus.
Nourish, sustain, and heal.
Help me according to your will.
May my dumb spirit testify,
my weakness mend,
my blind eyes see,
my heart rejoice.
  Lord, help me.   Amen.

57

22. When did we . . . ?

'When the Son of man comes in his glory, and all the angels with him, then he will sit on his glorious throne. Before him will be gathered all the nations, and he will separate them one from another as a shepherd separates the sheep from the goats, and he will place the sheep at his right hand, but the goats at the left. Then the King will say to those at his right hand, "Come, O blessed of my Father, inherit the kingdom prepared for you from the foundation of the world; for I was hungry and you gave me food, I was thirsty and you gave me drink, I was a stranger and you welcomed me, I was naked and you clothed me, I was sick and you visited me, I was in prison and you came to me.' Then the righteous will answer him, "Lord, when did we see thee hungry and feed thee, or thirsty and give thee drink? And when did we see thee a stranger and welcome thee, or naked and clothe thee? And when did we see thee sick or in prison and visit thee?" And the King will answer them, "Truly, I say to you, as you did it to one of the least of these my brethren, you did it to me." ' **Matthew 25: 31–40**

Lord Shaftesbury's funeral, 1885

It was raining. The procession made its way through crowded streets towards the Abbey. In Parliament Street, delegates from innumerable societies waited behind their banners to join it as it passed. But despite bands and banners it was a sad occasion, for those who watched were thinking of a friend whom they would not see again. They stood side by side on the pavement, at one for a brief moment in their love for a man who had loved them all; and then they went their different ways, peers of the realm and Piccadilly flower-girls; black-coated clerks and waifs from the London streets; seamstresses and chimney-sweeps and statesmen and clergymen; the costermongers who played the band and the boys from H.M.S. *Arethusa*. Thus London paid its tribute to the seventh Earl of Shaftesbury. . . .

Anthony Ashley Cooper, whom the world knew as Lord Ashley until his fiftieth year and who then succeeded his father as seventh Earl of Shaftesbury, dallied as a youth with the idea of studying science, but knew in his heart that his name and his inheritance marked him down for politics. In this sphere he had great and legitimate ambitions. He did not lack ability or influence or opportunity. He needed only to be somewhat more adaptable, rather more conventional in his regard for party ties, a little less truly himself, to have been a leader of the Tory party. But one by one he put these ambitions behind him. On his twenty-seventh birthday he wrote of his future career: 'The first principle God's honour, the second man's happiness, the means prayer and unremitting diligence.' To this recipe for a good life he remained faithful for fifty-odd years, deliberately devoting himself to helping others, by giving freely of himself to all who asked his aid and by inquiring ruthlessly into every injustice with which he came in contact.

Florence Higham

O God, the Father of heaven,
Have mercy upon us, miserable sinners.

And upon me,
'guilty of all the good I have not done.'
Teach me, Lord, how often righteousness
—holiness, even—
lies in 'doing' rather than simply 'not doing'.
Teach me to honour men and women who
have a Christian concern
for justice and fairness,
a Christian compassion for those in need.
As I read again these well-known words of Jesus,
open my eyes to see how strong they are.
      Jesus hungry; and I did—what?
      Jesus thirsty,
      Jesus friendless, lonely, shy even, a stranger,
      Jesus cold and poor and destitute,
      Jesus ill and a prisoner: and I did—what?

Help me to learn, this day,
and day by day,
those principles of which I read,
to which so many owed so much:
      'The first, God's honour
        the second, man's happiness,
          the means, prayer and unremitting diligence.'
Give me, *today*, the strength and grace, to make them mine.
Give me, *today*, some chance
to follow them in practice.

Lord, you have done so much for me, help me
to serve you in my brother's need today.
For your Name's sake.

Amen.

23. People like ourselves

So when Pilate saw that he was gaining nothing, but rather that a riot was beginning, he took water and washed his hands before the crowd, saying, 'I am innocent of this man's blood; see to it yourselves.' And all the people answered, 'His blood be on us and on our children!' Then he released for them Barabbas, and having scourged Jesus, delivered him to be crucified.

Then the soldiers of the governor took Jesus into the praetorium, and they gathered the whole battalion before him. And they stripped him and put a scarlet robe upon him, and plaiting a crown of thorns they put it on his head, and put a reed in his right hand. And kneeling before him they mocked him saying, 'Hail, King of the Jews!' And they spat upon him, and took the reed and struck him on the head. And when they had mocked him, they stripped him of the robe, and put his own clothes on him, and led him away to crucify him. . . . And when they had crucified him, they divided his garments among them by casting lots; then they sat down and kept watch over him there. And over his head they put the charge against him, which read, 'This is Jesus the King of the Jews.' Then two robbers were crucified with him, one on the right and one on the left. And those who passed by derided him. . . . So also the chief priests, with the scribes and elders, mocked him saying, 'He saved others; he cannot save himself.' . . . And the robbers who were crucified with him also reviled him in the same way.

Now from the sixth hour there was darkness over all the land until the ninth hour. And about the ninth hour Jesus cried with a loud voice, 'Eli, Eli, lama sabach-thani?' that is, 'My God, my God, why hast thou forsaken me?' And some of the bystanders hearing it said, 'This man is calling Elijah.' And one of them at once ran and took a sponge, filled it with vinegar, and put it on a reed, and gave it to him to drink. But the others said, 'Wait, let us see whether Elijah will come to save him.' And Jesus cried again with a loud voice and yielded up his spirit.

Matthew 27: 24–31, 35–39, 41, 42, 44–50

Sacred personages, living in a far-off land and time, using dignified rhythms of speech, making from time to time restrained gestures symbolic of brutality. They mocked and railed on Him and smote Him, they scourged and crucified Him. Well, they were people very remote from ourselves, and no doubt it was all done in the noblest and most beautiful manner. We should not like to think otherwise.

Unhappily, if we think about it at all, we must think otherwise. God was executed by people painfully like us, in a society very similar to our own—in the over-ripeness of the most splendid and sophisticated Empire the world has ever seen. In a nation famous for its religious genius and under a government renowned for its efficiency, He was executed by a corrupt church, a timid politician, and a fickle proletariat led by professional agitators. His executioners made vulgar jokes about Him, called him filthy names, taunted Him, smacked Him in the

face, flogged Him with the cat, and hanged Him on the common
gibbet—a bloody, dusty, sweaty, and sordid business.

Dorothy L. Sayers

O Christ, my Lord and friend,
you know how easily we think that, had we
known you then—
in the days of your earthly life, I mean—
we should have been among your most devoted followers.
        But should we? Should I?
Would I have found the faith to believe in you at the beginning?
Or the courage to follow an unknown wandering
anti-establishment prophet?
Would I have liked your politics, your reformation of
the religion I had learned as a child?
Would I have liked your teaching, your hard words,
the company you kept?
        I doubt it, Lord.

And as I read anew this shocking story, this account
which angels must weep to read,
I find it all so understandable.
        It could happen today, Lord—any day.
And which of the actors wears my face, I wonder?
I see myself in many of them. That description
rings all too true:
        'a corrupt church,
        a timid politician,
        a fickle proletariat.'
And because of them, the blood and dust and sweat,
the lash and thorns, the nails and spear, the pain and
sickness, the agony and death.
And because of them, I go free. I know forgiveness.
I have you as my friend.

Make me the sort of friend you need: the sort you needed then.
So let it be.
Amen.

61

24. The third day

When it was evening, there came a rich man from Arimathea, named Joseph, who also was a disciple of Jesus. He went to Pilate and asked for the body of Jesus. Then Pilate ordered it to be given to him. And Joseph took the body, and wrapped it in a clean linen shroud, and laid it in his own new tomb, which he had hewn in the rock; and he rolled a great stone to the door of the tomb, and departed. Mary Magdalene and the other Mary were there, sitting opposite the sepulchre.

Next day, that is, after the day of Preparation, the chief priests and the Pharisees gathered before Pilate and said, 'Sir, we remember how that impostor said, while he was still alive, "After three days I will rise again." Therefore order the sepulchre to be made secure until the third day, lest his disciples go and steal him away, and tell the people, "He has risen from the dead," and the last fraud will be worse than the first.' Pilate said to them, 'You have a guard of soldiers; go, make it as secure as you can.' So they went and made the sepulchre secure by sealing the stone and setting a guard.

Now after the sabbath, toward the dawn of the first day of the week, Mary Magdalene and the other Mary went to see the sepulchre. And behold, there was a great earthquake; for an angel of the Lord descended from heaven and came and rolled back the stone, and sat upon it. His appearance was like lightning, and his raiment white as snow. And for fear of him the guards trembled and became like dead men. But the angel said to the women, 'Do not be afraid, for I know that you seek Jesus who was crucified. He is not here; for he has risen, as he said. Come, see the place where he lay.

Matthew 27: 57–28: 6

Easter Night

All night had shout of men and cry
    Of woeful women filled His way;
Until that noon of sombre sky
    On Friday, clamour and display
Smote Him; no solitude had He,
No silence, since Gethsemane.

Public was Death; but Power, but Might,
    But Life again, but Victory,
Were hushed within the dead of night,
    The shutter'd dark, the secrecy.
And all alone, alone, alone,
He rose again behind the stone.

Alice Meynell

Easter Day

Death and darkness, get you packing,
Nothing now to man is lacking,
All your triumphs now are ended,
And what Adam marred, is mended.

Henry Vaughan

My Lord Jesus,
I come in my thoughts to Joseph's tomb.
The cool darkness: the great stone shutting out the world
from this private place: the guard of soldiers: the
official seal.
And your poor broken body, at rest after the pain, the
indignities, the clamour, the agony of spirit.
At rest. Your work done.
And there, with time standing still, and the angels waiting
with bated breath—what happens?
In a word, Resurrection.

A new kind of body: a risen life: the power of God
present, in what Fatherly love and gladness,
to put an end to the power of death,
and to restore you, my Lord
—more than restore—
to fullness of life eternal.
In a line:
'Death and darkness, get you packing'!
And as I sense the awe of that first Easter morning,
so let the meaning of Easter fill my heart.
You know my heart, Lord—
jaded, not easily moved,
all too ready to have heard it all before.

But move it now
        move it in awe and reverence for those Easter days,
        move it in gratitude for your broken body, your shed blood,
        move it in joy—deep-down, utterly convinced, sober *joy*—
and let me keep my Easter all year round, as a Christian should.

For your sake, who died for me and rose again.
Amen.

63

25. Healers

Now Simon's mother-in-law lay sick with a fever, and immediately they told him of her. And he came and took her by the hand and lifted her up, and the fever left her; and she served them.

That evening, at sundown, they brought to him all who were sick or possessed with demons. And the whole city was gathered together about the door. And he healed many who were sick with various diseases, and cast out many demons; and he would not permit the demons to speak, because they knew him.

And in the morning, a great while before day, he rose and went out to a lonely place, and there he prayed. And Simon and those who were with him followed him, and they found him and said to him, 'Every one is searching for you.' And he said to them, 'Let us go on to the next towns, that I may preach there also; for that is why I came out.' And he went throughout all Galilee, preaching in their synagogues and casting out demons.

Mark 1: 30–39

To a young physician,
with Doré's picture of Christ healing the sick

So stood of old the holy Christ
    Amidst the suffering throng;
With whom His lightest touch sufficed
    To make the weakest strong.

That healing gift He lends to them
    Who use it in His name;
The power that filled His garment's hem
    Is evermore the same. . . .

The holiest task by Heaven decreed,
    An errand all divine,
The burden of our common need
    To render less is thine.

The paths of pain are thine. Go forth
    With patience, trust, and hope;
The sufferings of a sin-sick earth
    Shall give thee ample scope.

Beside the unveiled mysteries
    Of life and death go stand,
With guarded lips and reverent eyes
    And pure of heart and hand.

So shalt thou be with power endued
From Him who went about
The Syrian hillsides doing good,
And casting demons out.

That Good Physician liveth yet
Thy friend and guide to be;
The Healer by Gennesaret
Shall walk the rounds with thee.
John Greenleaf Whittier

My Lord, what an evening!

'The whole city gathered together about the door.'
Poor old men, bent old women, crippled children—dying even—
lame, blind, withered, diseased,
full of pain, weariness, weakness
—and full of demons too.
And you healed many—just as you healed the leper:
and I thank you that this healing gift is with us still.

I thank you for the power of recuperation.
What is it the doctors say?—that they have no
power to heal, but only to help create the conditions in which
nature can do the work.
Nature? *Your* Nature: *your* healing principle
implanted in creation. *Your* healing gift wherever it is found.

And so I pray for those who are ill, remembering
what it feels like
in the lesser illnesses I've known.
Be Lord of their pain: and be their joy even in weakness.
And I pray for doctors—overworked, gentle, much-tried
fallible men. And nurses, with their own troubles,
their difficult patients, and big responsibilities.
And for those who have no doctors: for whom
pain is not something to be relieved,
but to be borne.
I pray for them.
Oh, and I thank you that I live in the age of anaesthetics!
Grant, Lord, that as we learn the secrets of your healing gifts,
we may learn also the wisdom to use them well.
For your Name's sake. Amen.

26. A beautiful thing

And while he was at Bethany in the house of Simon the leper, as he sat at table, a woman came with an alabaster jar of ointment of pure nard, very costly, and she broke the jar and poured it over his head. But there were some who said to themselves indignantly, 'Why was the ointment thus wasted? For this ointment might have been sold for more than three hundred denarii, and given to the poor.' And they reproached her. But Jesus said, 'Let her alone: why do you trouble her? She has done a beautiful thing to me. For you always have the poor with you, and whenever you will, you can do good to them; but you will not always have me. She has done what she could; she has anointed my body beforehand for burying. And truly, I say to you, wherever the gospel is preached in the whole world, what she has done will be told in memory of her.'

Then Judas Iscariot, who was one of the twelve, went to the chief priests in order to betray him to them. And when they heard it they were glad, and promised to give him money. And he sought an opportunity to betray him.

Mark 14: 3–11

Betty Barton

'Close to the pulpit, and present at every service sat Betty Barton, with eyes lifted up to the preacher, drinking in every word he said. She could neither read nor write, but her soul was on fire with love for her Saviour and the souls for whom He died. She made it her business to inform the clergy of every case of sickness in her neighbourhood, of new families coming into the district, of children who were ready for baptism, or who were attending no Sunday school. Sitting at the door of her shop, when she saw one of the clergymen near, she would beckon to him. 'Curate, there's a man in yon house whom ye might go to see.' Or, 'Have ye called lately on so-and-so? It would pay thee to go there.' When the Ragged School was opened, she appeared Sunday after Sunday leading a child in each hand whom she had picked out of the gutter. She even sometimes would take a class: she could not read, but she could tell the little mites around her stories out of the Bible. She did what she could. She has received her reward. May I be as near to the Lord as she will be when He comes again!

J. B. Lancelot

Thank you, Lord,
for all those whose love for you
beams clear and bright.
Thank you for that woman in the gospel
whose gift of love ('so wasteful, so extravagant'!)
is still remembered
across the world and down the ages—
a beautiful thing for Jesus.

And thank you for Betty Barton
—how surprised she would have been
to find her name in print!—
and all the faithful women of your church
(many more women than men, it always seems)
who loved much: and in their own homes
and streets and neighbourhoods
were full of love for Jesus.
I think of some I've known: old Mrs Lapslie,
deaf as a post, poor as a church mouse,
full of joy and peace in believing.

O Christ,
how soon our love for you is
taken for granted.
How soon our love for others becomes
professional.
Keep me from resenting the uninhibited love
some others show.
Let me rejoice in every
beautiful thing for Jesus.
Let me even love enough
day by day
that when the moment comes
it may be so of me
that 'I did what I could'—
beginning now.

Amen.

27. Loving

And behold, a lawyer stood up to put him to the test, saying, 'Teacher what shall I do to inherit eternal life?' He said to him, 'What is written in the law? How do you read?' And he answered, 'You shall love the Lord your God with all your heart, and with all your soul, and with all your strength, and with all your mind; and your neighbour as yourself.' And he said to him, 'You have answered right; do this, and you will live.'

But he, desiring to justify himself, said to Jesus, 'And who is my neighbour?' Jesus replied, 'A man was going down from Jerusalem to Jericho, and he fell among robbers, who stripped him and beat him and departed, leaving him half dead. Now by chance a priest was going down that road; and when he saw him he passed by on the other side. So likewise a Levite, when he came to the place and saw him, passed by on the other side. But a Samaritan, as he journeyed, came to where he was; and when he saw him, he had compassion, and went to him and bound up his wounds, pouring on oil and wine; then he set him on his own beast and brought him to an inn, and took care of him. And the next day he took out two denarii and gave them to the innkeeper, saying, "Take care of him; and whatever more you spend, I will repay you when I come back." Which of these three, do you think, proved neighbour to the man who fell among the robbers?' He said, 'The one who showed mercy on him,' And Jesus said to him, 'Go and do likewise.'

Luke 10: 25–37

Who is my neighbour?

Granted, loving means giving and serving. But *what* shall we give? *How* shall we serve? The Good Samaritan parable answers this question for us too, because evidently the Samaritan's service was determined by the man's need. He had been brutally assaulted by thieves, and left naked, bleeding, destitute, half dead. There was no question that his urgent need was medical care. So the Samaritan dressed his wounds, rode him to the nearest inn, took care of him there and paid the innkeeper for any further treatment he would need. The one thing the Samaritan did not do was preach to him! He put oil and wine into his wounds; he did not stuff tracts into his pockets.

Our evangelical neglect of social concern until recent years, and the whole argument about evangelism and social action, has been as unseemly as it has been unnecessary. Of course evangelical Christians have quite rightly rejected the so-called 'social gospel' (which replaces the good news of salvation with a message of social amelioration), but it is incredible that we should ever have set evangelistic and social work over against each other as alternatives. Both should be authentic expressions of neighbour-love. For who is my neighbour, whom I am to love? He is neither a bodyless soul, nor a soulless body, nor a private individual divorced from a social environment. God made man a physical, spiritual and social being. My neighbour is a body-soul-in community. I cannot claim to love my neighbour if I'm really concerned

68

for only one aspect of him, whether his soul or his body or his community.

John Stott

Dear God, I sometimes think
I could be very happy with you—
and with my friends of course—
if I had fewer 'neighbours' to consider.
I sometimes wonder if I know
what it means to love: indeed
if there is any action I have ever done
which, in the last analysis,
was not a selfish one.

'Loving means giving and serving'—that
must be right.
I may not be able to love to order, in
the sense of 'feel love', but I can
give and serve.
And Jesus' story is about
giving and serving, and he finished it: 'Go
and do likewise.'

Dear God, I will. And I will start
with . . .
Not because I feel like it, but because Jesus
commands it.
'Who is my neighbour?' He is, and she is.
Let me be neighbour too to them.

And as I serve, and give, let me learn too.
Let me learn what it means, to see another as a
'body-soul-in-community'
and as a person.
Teach me to do it, and to learn love by doing.
For Christ's sake.

Amen.

28. Father and son

And he said, 'There was a man who had two sons; and the younger of them said to his father, 'Father, give me the share of property that falls to me.'' And he divided his living between them. Not many days later, the younger son gathered all he had and took his journey into a far country, and there he squandered his property in loose living. And when he had spent everything, a great famine arose in that country, and he began to be in want. So he went and joined himself to one of the citizens of that country, who sent him into his fields to feed swine. And he would gladly have fed on the pods that the swine ate; and no one gave him anything. But when he came to himself he said, "How many of my father's hired servants have bread enough and to spare, but I perish here with hunger! I will arise and go to my father, and I will say to him, 'Father, I have sinned against heaven and before you; I am no longer worthy to be called your son; treat me as one of your hired servants.' "

And he arose and came to his father. But while he was yet at a distance, his father saw him and had compassion, and ran and embraced him and kissed him. And the son said to him, "Father, I have sinned against heaven and before you; I am no longer worthy to be called your son." But the father said to his servants, "Bring quickly the best robe, and put it on him; and put a ring on his hand, and shoes on his feet; and bring the fatted calf and kill it, and let us eat and make merry; for this my son was dead, and is alive again; he was lost, and is found." And they began to make merry.'

Luke 15: 11–24

The Alchemist

My Master an elixir hath that turns
All base and worthless substances to gold.
From rubble stones He fashions palaces
Most beautiful and stately to behold.
He garners with a craftsman's skilled care
All that we break, and weeping cast away.
His eyes see uncut opals in the rock
And shapely vessels in our trampled clay.
The sum of life's lost opportunities.
The broken friendships, and the wasted years.
These are His raw materials; His hands
Rest on the fragments, weld them with His tears.

A patient Alchemist!—He bides His time
Broods while the south winds breathe, the North winds blow,
And weary self, at enmity with self,
Works out its own destruction, bitter slow.
Then when our dreams have dwindled into smoke
Our gallant highways petered out in mire,
Our airy castles crumbled into dust,
Leaving us stripped of all save fierce desire,

He comes, with feet deliberate and slow,
Who counts a contrite heart His sacrifice.
(No other bidders rise to stake their claims,
He only on our ruins sets a price.)
And stooping very low engraves with care
His Name, indelible, upon our dust;
And from the ashes of our self-despair
Kindles a flame of hope and humble trust,
He seeks no second site on which to build,
But on the old foundation, stone by stone,
Cementing sad experience with grace,
Fashions a stronger temple of His own.

Patricia St John

Father, I love this story.

Help me to read it sometimes with new eyes:
not just 'The Prodigal Son', on which I've
often taught a Bible class:
not *him* but *me*.

My prayer like his is 'Give me'.
Like him, I cherish independence.
I know that feeling, that freedom only comes
when we break loose and move away.
How often do I plan my course, seeing things
only from the point of view of what I want, and not
the needs and wants of others?
'The sum of life's lost opportunities'—not something
which I think of much: perhaps I should.
And you, my Father—you are in this story.
You had another son—or millions more. What
could I mean to you, among so many?
Why not
forget the whole thing, forget you ever made me,
and start again?

'He seeks no second site on which to build.'
No-one could take my place
in the heart and family of God.
Thank you, Father. That makes me merry too!

Amen.

29. Treasure in heaven

He also said to the disciples, 'There was a rich man who had a steward, and charges were brought to him that this man was wasting his goods. And he called him and said to him, "What is this that I hear about you? Turn in the account of your stewardship, for you can no longer be steward." And the steward said to himself, "What shall I do, since my master is taking the stewardship away from me? I am not strong enough to dig, and I am ashamed to beg. I have decided what to do, so that people may receive me into their houses when I am put out of the stewardship." So, summoning his master's debtors one by one, he said to the first, "How much do you owe my master?" He said, "A hundred measures of oil." And he said to him, "Take your bill, and sit down quickly and write fifty." Then he said to another, "And how much do you owe?" He said, "A hundred measures of wheat." He said to him, "Take your bill, and write eighty." The master commended the dishonest steward for his prudence; for the sons of this world are wiser in their own generation than the sons of light. And I tell you, make friends for yourselves by means of unrighteous mammon, so that when it fails they may receive you into the eternal habitations.'

Luke 16: 1–9

When we are faced, through the challenging words of Jesus, with the necessity of laying up for ourselves 'treasures in heaven', we are apt to think that this is a very difficult thing to do, involving years of painful self-discipline and 'character training'. This is a false idea, for the essential thing in Christianity is making friends with Jesus Christ, and the true 'treasures in heaven' are simply this friendship with God in Christ. Jesus called men into this friendship. 'Henceforth I call you not servants ... but friends.' The *'true riches'* spoken of in this parable are nothing more than the friendship of God in Jesus Christ. The heavenly treasure does not lie in the moral character we form within our present personality through stern discipline of will and emotion or anything like that. Such 'righteousness' will be shown up as 'filthy rags' in the day of crisis. To lay up heavenly riches means to come now to Jesus Christ in personal trust and love. This friendship will abide for ever.

Jesus, in passing, urges that if a man is wise, he will put even his material resources into this matter of the service of God. *'Make to yourselves friends of the mammon of unrighteousness.'* All reliable commentators are agreed that Jesus in these words is calling for a wise stewardship of money in His service. That money is usually an evil thing is freely admitted here by Jesus. He calls it the *'mammon of unrighteousness'*. It is the source of trouble and strife on the earth. It causes wars, murders, hatreds, family quarrels. It is a tainted evil thing, and yet it can be made the instrument for forming those relationships that will last into the world beyond. The unjust steward made friends with his lord's money, using it to bind human hearts to himself. Filthy stolen money it was, but his action gives us a hint of what money can do in the service of God. Happy is the man who learns that by the grace of God, not only his brains and his energy and his imagination can be thrown into the service of God for an everlasting purpose, but also his money.

R. S. Wallace

Jesus my friend,
I thank you that your friendship lasts for ever:
that it grows deeper and stronger as the years pass.
I thank you for the hope of heaven—
which I cannot really imagine but in which
I firmly trust and on which my stake is put.
Help me to begin now to stockpile
heavenly treasure,
rather as a bride in the old days had her bottom drawer
steadily filling with what she would need
for her new life.

What are my treasures—the things I value most?
How do they fare when it comes to the last journey of all?
In a word—do they really belong to this world: so that
they stay in it when I leave it?
Or do they belong to the world to come—though
some have their beginnings now?

Mostly, I guess, mine belong here.
So I pray *today*, while there is time, that you will wean me
from holding earthly treasures, however good,
as closest to my heart.

Increase my appetite for heavenly treasure
        the knowledge of God,
        the friendship of Jesus,
        the life of the Spirit,
so that the ties that hold my heart to this present world
begin to loosen—
for where my treasure is, there is my heart also.
And what I ask for myself, help me to seek also
for my friends,
with all the shrewdness of this steward, dishonest though he was!
For your Name's sake. Amen.

30. My name is Dives

There was a rich man, who was clothed in purple and fine linen and who feasted sumptuously every day. And at his gate lay a poor man named Lazarus, full of sores, who desired to be fed with what fell from the rich man's table; moreover the dogs came and licked his sores. The poor man died and was carried by the angels to Abraham's bosom. The rich man also died and was buried; and in Hades, being in torment, he lifted up his eyes, and saw Abraham far off and Lazarus in his bosom. And he called out, "Father Abraham, have mercy upon me, and send Lazarus to dip the end of his finger in water and cool my tongue; for I am in anguish in this flame." But Abraham said, "Son, remember that you in your lifetime received your good things, and Lazarus in like manner evil things; but now he is comforted here, and you are in anguish. And besides all this, between us and you a great chasm has been fixed, in order that those who would pass from here to you may not be able, and none may cross from there to us." And he said, "Then I beg you, father, to send him to my father's house, for I have five brothers, so that he may warn them, lest they also come into this place of torment." But Abraham said, "They have Moses and the prophets; let them hear them." And he said, "No, father Abraham; but if some one goes to them from the dead, they will repent." He said to him, "If they do not hear Moses and the prophets, neither will they be convinced if some one should rise from the dead." '

Luke 16: 19–31

The rich man ... possessed everything that life has to offer, but which it offers only as a loan and demands back again when a man departs forever. Now he sits there in dreadful loneliness which he was so clever to conceal in life, and across the appalling distance he sees the transfiguration of Lazarus. What a contrast!

To see this is really what hell is. For to be in hell simply means to be utterly separated from God, but in such a way that one is compelled to see him, that one must see him as a thirsty man sees a silvery spring from which he dare not drink. This is hell: to be forced to see the glory of God and have no access to it.

And yet the life of even the most godless man is different from hell in two important respects.

First, here on earth the rich man, the godless man, is able to hide from himself his true condition. Life provides all kinds of astonishingly effective anodynes and narcotics, all of which are nothing but misused gifts of God. But now in hell, that is, beyond a fixed boundary set by God, all the securities and safeguards disappear into thin air. What here is only a tiny flame of secret self-reproach that flickers up occasionally and is quickly smothered, there becomes a scorching fire. What here is no more than a slight ticking sound in our conscience suddenly becomes the trumpet tone of judgment which can no longer be ignored. Lazarus is permitted to see what he believed, but the rich man is compelled to see what he did *not* believe.

74

Second, inevitably comes the time when all the decisions have been made. Here God is still calling us, and *we* are the ones to speak. But one day God will open the books and *he* will be the one to speak. Here Jesus Christ is asking us whether we will have him as our 'one consolation in life and death.' But one day this pleading, comforting question will cease to be asked. The mercy of God is boundless, yes; but it is not offered indefinitely. Here we are still living by the grace of God and the merit of Christ; the sentence is still punctuated with a colon. We still have a reprieve, a season of grace; we still have time to live and turn back home. But one day comes—finality, period.

Helmut Thielicke

O God, my Father,
my name is Dives,
one of the many nameless rich,
who had it all here, and nothing left for the hereafter.
How rich I am!

Not as the banks count riches, perhaps
(though I suppose in standard of living
I must be better off than nineteen twentieths
of the human family):
But in opportunity, in education, in freedom,
comfort, pleasure, in what makes life, as we say
'worth living'
rather than a mere struggle for hard existence.
And so my name is Dives.

And yet I call myself a godly man—
not holy, of course, but one in touch with God.
The grace of God and the work of Christ avail for me.
Make me, then, a new kind of Dives:
a Dives concerned for my brother Lazarus:
a Dives who knows this life is short, preliminary,
held in trust:
a Dives who cares today for all his brothers
(the rich five, and the world's poor alike),
a Dives ready to reckon all things loss
(even the good things God has given me)
compared with Christ, his call and service.
So let it be.

Amen.

31. First principles

In the beginning was the Word, and the Word was with God, and the Word was God. He was in the beginning with God; all things were made through him, and without him was not anything made that was made. In him was life, and the life was the light of men. The light shines in the darkness, and the darkness has not overcome it.

There was a man sent from God, whose name was John. He came for testimony, to bear witness to the light, that all might believe through him. He was not the light, but came to bear witness to the light.

The true light that enlightens every man was coming into the world. He was in the world, and the world was made through him, yet the world knew him not. He came to his own home, and his own people received him not. But to all who received him, who believed in his name, he gave power to become children of God; who were born, not of blood nor of the will of the flesh nor of the will of man, but of God.

And the Word became flesh and dwelt among us, full of grace and truth; we have beheld his glory, glory as of the only Son from the Father.

(John bore witness to him, and cried, 'This was he of whom I said, 'He who comes after me ranks before me, for he was before me.') And from his fullness have we all received, grace upon grace. For the law was given through Moses; grace and truth came through Jesus Christ. No one has ever seen God; the only Son, who is in the bosom of the Father, he has made him known.

John 1: 1–18

Liberalism

Whenever men are able to act at all, there is the chance of extreme and intemperate action; and therefore, when there is exercise of mind, there is the chance of wayward or mistaken exercise. Liberty of thought is in itself a good; but it gives an opening to false liberty. Now by Liberalism I mean false liberty of thought, or the exercise of thought upon matters, in which, from the constitution of the human mind, thought cannot be brought to any successful issue, and therefore is out of place. Among such matters are first principles of whatever kind; and of these the most sacred and momentous are especially to be reckoned the truths of Revelation. Liberalism then is the mistake of subjecting to human judgment those revealed doctrines which are in their nature beyond and independent of it, and of claiming to determine on intrinsic grounds the truth and value of propositions which rest for their reception simply on the eternal authority of the Divine Word.

J. H. Newman

O living God
whose living Word,
your Son, Jesus Christ, our Lord,
is from everlasting to everlasting,
God, with God, and yet made flesh
in space and time
to live a man among us,
the light and life of men:

O living and eternal God,
who stands revealed
in Jesus,
I come before you, finite, empty, sinful,
and yet your child.
        What can I know
except what you declare
and enable me to grasp and understand?
        What can I have
except what you choose to give me?
        What can I be
but what your love and wisdom make me?

O God my Father,
let me then rest on your
self-revelation:
my faith called forth in response to
your divine Word;
let me find all my security within your
enfolding love:
that Christ in me may be still today
a Light shining in darkness:
and I, like John, a witness
to that Light.

I ask it in Christ's Name.

Amen.

32. Telling Jesus

On the third day there was a marriage at Cana in Galilee, and the mother of Jesus was there; Jesus also was invited to the marriage, with his disciples. When the wine failed, the mother of Jesus said to him, 'They have no wine.' And Jesus said to her, 'O woman, what have you to do with me? My hour has not yet come.' His mother said to the servants, 'Do whatever he tells you.' Now six stone jars were standing there, for the Jewish rites of purification, each holding twenty or thirty gallons. Jesus said to them, 'Fill the jars with water.' And they filled them up to the brim. He said to them, 'Now draw some out, and take it to the steward of the feast.' So they took it. When the steward of the feast tasted the water now become wine, and did not know where it came from (though the servants who had drawn the water knew), the steward of the feast called the bridegroom and said to him, 'Every man serves the good wine first; and when men have drunk freely, then the poor wine; but you have kept the good wine until now.'

John 2: 1–10

This secret of prayer became very plain to me once many years ago as I was reading the delightful little account of the wedding in Cana of Galilee.

Jesus, His mother, and His disciples were bidden to the wedding. In all likelihood the family was closely related to, or very friendly with, the family of Jesus. At least, we notice that the host and hostess had acquainted the mother of Jesus with the embarrassing situation which had arisen when the wine had given out.

Whereupon the mother of Jesus reveals herself as a tried and true woman of prayer.

In the first place, she goes to the right place with the need she has become acquainted with. She goes to Jesus and tells Him everything.

In the next place, notice what she says to Jesus. Just these few, simple words, 'They have no wine.' Note here what prayer is. To pray is to tell Jesus what we lack. Intercession is to tell Jesus what we see that others lack.

In the third place, let us notice that she did nothing more. When she had told Jesus about the need of her friends, she knew that she did not have to do any more about it. She knew that she did not have to help Him either by suggesting what He should do or anything else. She knew Him and knew that this need had been left in the proper hands. She knew that He Himself knew what He wanted to do. She knew also that she did not have to influence Him or persuade Him to give these friends a helping hand. No one is so willing to help as He is!

In the fourth place, let us notice that when the mother of Jesus had presented her petition, she had done her part. As far as she was concerned she was through with the matter, she had left it with Him. She was no longer responsible, so to speak, for the embarrassing situation. The responsibility had been placed upon Jesus.

O. Hallesby

My Father,
make me a Christian concerned for those who are my friends.
Not *only* them of course, not a closed circle,
but all the same,
a kind of family.
And, concerned for them and their well-being,
make me an intercessor for them.
You know how quickly my prayers go all
soft-centred.
'Bless Jack,' I say: 'Bless Jill.'

I suppose that is why, where it can be had,
real prayer needs information to sustain it.
That's why we have all those missionary magazines,
those prayer letters, diaries, cards.
Teach me to learn a lesson from this story,
to lift my friends into your presence,
with their real needs:
to bring to your omnipotence a human need—
('They have no wine!')
and not a programme by which it may be met.

So, Lord, I look again at that little list
of friends. I see that if I am to intercede
intelligently, obediently,
I need to know a bit more, imagine a bit more, think
a bit more—and I suppose all those really mean
love a bit more
so that I can bring their real need to you.

You know them, of course, from the beginning,
but this seems to be the way you offer us
—indeed, command us—
to share in one another's life and work and need.

Help me to do my part.
I need your help in this.
Begin to meet my need.
For your Name's sake.
Amen.

33. Believing and coming

Jesus said to them, 'I am the bread of life; he who comes to me shall not hunger, and he who believes in me shall never thirst. But I said to you that you have seen me and yet do not believe. All that the Father gives me will come to me; and him who comes to me I will not cast out. For I have come down from heaven, not to do my own will, but the will of him who sent me; and this is the will of him who sent me, that I should lose nothing of all that he has given me, but raise it up at the last day. For this is the will of my Father, that every one who sees the Son and believes in him should have eternal life; and I will raise him up at the last day.'

The Jews then murmured at him, because he said, 'I am the bread which came down from heaven.' They said, 'Is not this Jesus, the son of Joseph, whose father and mother we know? How does he now say, "I have come down from heaven"?' Jesus answered them, 'Do not murmur among yourselves. No one can come to me unless the Father who sent me draws him; and I will raise him up at the last day. It is written in the prophets, "And they shall all be taught by God." Every one who has heard and learned from the Father comes to me. Not that any one has seen the Father except him who is from God; he has seen the Father. Truly, truly, I say to you, he who believes has eternal life. I am the bread of life. Your fathers ate the manna in the wilderness, and they died. This is the bread which comes down from heaven, that a man may eat of it and not die. I am the living bread which came down from heaven; if any one eats of this bread, he will live for ever; and the bread which I shall give for the life of the world is my flesh.'

John 6: 35–51

True Christian faith rests on content. It is not a vague thing which takes the place of real understanding, nor is it the strength of belief which is of value. *The true basis for faith is not the faith itself, but the work which Christ finished on the cross.* My believing is not the basis for being saved—the basis is the work of Christ. Christian faith is turned outward to an objective person: 'Believe on the Lord Jesus, and thou shalt be saved.' ...

What does it mean to believe on, to cast oneself on, Christ? I would suggest there are four crucial aspects to be considered. More detail could be considered, but these are crucial. They are not slogans to be repeated by rote and they do not have to be said in these words, but the individual must have come to a positive conclusion and affirmation concerning them, if he is to believe in the biblical sense:

1. Do you believe that God exists and that he is a personal God, and that Jesus Christ is God—remembering that we are not talking of the *word* or *idea* god, but of the infinite-personal God who is there?
2. Do you acknowledge that you are guilty in the presence of this God—remembering that we are not talking about guilt feelings, but true moral guilt?
3. Do you believe that Jesus Christ died in space and time in history

on the cross, and that when He died His substitutional work of bearing God's punishment against sin was fully accomplished and complete?
4. On the basis of God's promises in His written communication to us, the Bible, do you (or have you) cast yourself on this Christ as your personal Saviour—not trusting in anything you yourself have ever done or ever will do?

But note with care that God's promise: 'He that believes on the Son has everlasting life', rests upon: God's being there; Christ being the second person of the Trinity whose death therefore has infinite value; my not coming presumptuously in thinking I can save myself, but casting myself on the finished work of Christ and the written promises of God. My faith is simply the empty hands by which I accept God's free gift.

Francis Schaeffer

Jesus, my bread of life,
without whom there is no fulfilment—
only hunger and exhaustion and weakness
and death:
Jesus, my living bread, given for the life of men,
in flesh and blood
—the body broken and the blood poured out—
that I too may live and not die:
Lord, I believe and I rejoice!

I rejoice too, Jesus my Lord and Saviour,
that he who comes to you,
you will never turn away—
and those who cast themselves upon you,
you will not cast out,
For where had I been otherwise,
Jesus my Lord?

Jesus, that you are there: not in
imagination, not in myth or story,
but there; truly there:
Jesus, that your work is finished,
my redemption paid,
paid, accomplished, done:
Jesus, that you receive sinners,
that you love them, and put them right:
Jesus, my bread of life, my wine of joy,
thank you for all you are. Amen.

34. None righteous?

Jesus answered them, 'Truly, truly, I say to you, every one who commits sin is a slave to sin. The slave does not continue in the house for ever; the son continues for ever. So if the Son makes you free, you will be free indeed. I know that you are descendants of Abraham; yet you seek to kill me, because my word finds no place in you. I speak of what I have seen with my Father, and you do what you have heard from your father.'

They answered him. 'Abraham is our father.' Jesus said to them, 'If you were Abraham's children, you would do what Abraham did, but now you seek to kill me, a man who has told you the truth which I heard from God; this is not what Abraham did. You do what your father did.' They said to him, 'We were not born of fornication; we have one Father, even God.' Jesus said to them, 'If God were your Father, you would love me, for I proceeded and came forth from God; I came not of my own accord, but he sent me. Why do you not understand what I say? It is because you cannot bear to hear my word. You are of your father the devil, and your will is to do your father's desires. He was a murderer from the beginning, and has nothing to do with the truth, because there is no truth in him. When he lies, he speaks according to his own nature, for he is a liar and the father of lies. But, because I tell the truth, you do not believe me. Which of you convicts me of sin? If I tell the truth, why do you not believe me? He who is of God hears the words of God; the reason why you do not hear them is that you are not of God.'

John 8: 34–47

To prove a negative is always difficult; to prove it absolutely often an impossibility. It is obviously an impossibility absolutely to demonstrate that the life and character of any man are entirely stainless. But in the case of Jesus the witness is as strong as the very nature of the thing to be proved can possibly admit. His enemies are witnesses to it. With all their ingenuity of hate and malice, never once did they dare to prefer against Him any moral charge, and insinuations such as that 'this man receiveth sinners and eateth with them' fell harmless upon Him. His friends are witnesses. They described Him as 'separate from sinners.' They were orthodox Jews, steeped in the doctrine that 'there is none righteous, no, not one.' But they were compelled to contradict themselves. 'Yes, one,' they said against their scriptures; '*He* did no sin.' And we too are witnesses of the stainless perfection of the character of Jesus. For His friends have given us about Him far more than a vague eulogy. They have given us accounts, short indeed but particularised, of His life. They do not merely affirm His stainlessness, which were easy. They exhibit it, which it were simply impossible to do except from the life. We have there what Jesus said and did in all kinds of circumstances and on all manner of occasions—in public and private, in the sunshine of success and the gloom of failure, in the houses of His friends and in face of His foes, in life and in the last great trial of death. It is the detailed picture of a man who never made a false step, never said the word that ought not to have been said, never, in short, fell below perfection. Such a portrait is of necessity a true portrait. It simply cannot be an idealised picture. That which is so above human criticism is not less above our conception.

P. Carnegie Simpson

'Depart from me,
for I am a sinful man, O Lord'—

If I have never understood what
Peter felt that day
I begin to understand it now.
How *can* a man walk through this world
living a very public sort of life
and do no sin?
What distance must separate him
from me?

What was your secret, Lord?
Not freedom from temptation, that I know.
Your temptations were
akin to mine but on
a larger scale.
It must be in the secret places
of the will, and in the desires
of the heart,
that your victories were won,
your will delighting in the Father's will
and in the Father's voice.

Keep my heart open to those 'words of God'
which are your words to me.
So that in loving I may
want to listen:
listening may want to understand:
and understanding may obey my Father's will.
You know, Lord, what it is
to be a man like me.
Make me to know more of what it is
to be like you.

For your Name's sake.
Amen.

35. From death to life

They brought to the Pharisees the man who had formerly been blind. Now it was a sabbath day when Jesus made the clay and opened his eyes. The Pharisees again asked him how he had received his sight. And he said to them, 'He put clay on my eyes, and I washed, and I see.' Some of the Pharisees said, 'This man is not from God, for he does not keep the sabbath.' But others said, 'How can a man who is a sinner do such signs?' There was a division among them. So they again said to the blind man, 'What do you say about him, since he has opened your eyes?' He said, 'He is a prophet.'

The Jews did not believe that he had been blind and had received his sight, until they called the parents of the man who had received his sight, and asked them, 'Is this your son, who you say was born blind? How then does he now see?' His parents answered, 'We know that this is our son, and that he was born blind: but how he now sees we do not know, nor do we know who opened his eyes. Ask him; he is of age, he will speak for himself.' His parents said this because they feared the Jews, for the Jews had already agreed that if any one should confess him to be Christ, he was to be put out of the synagogue. Therefore his parents said, 'He is of age, ask him.'

So for the second time they called the man who had been blind, and said to him, 'Give God the praise; we know that this man is a sinner.' He answered, 'Whether he is a sinner, I do not know; one thing I know, that though I was blind, now I see.'

John 9: 13–25

'The parson is converted'

Thursday, Friday, and Saturday passed by, each day and night more dark and despairing than the preceding one. On the Sunday, I was so ill that I was quite unfit to take the service. Mr Aitken had said to me, 'If I were you, I would shut the church, and say to the congregation, "I will not preach again till I am converted. Pray for me!" ' Shall I do this?

The sun was shining brightly, and before I could make up my mind to put off the service, the bells struck out a merry peal, and sent their summons far away over the hills. Now the thought came to me that I would go to church and read the morning prayers, and after that dismiss the people.... And while I was reading the Gospel, I thought, well, I will just say a few words in explanation of this, and then I will dismiss them. So I went up into the pulpit and gave out my text. I took it from the gospel of the day—'What think ye of Christ?' (Matthew 22: 42).

As I went on to explain the passage, I saw that the Pharisees and scribes did not know that Christ was the Son of God, or that He was come to save them. They were looking for a king, the son of David, to reign over them as they were. Something was telling me, all the time, 'You are no better than the Pharisees yourself—you do not believe that He is the Son of God, and that He is come to save you, any more than they did.' I do not remember all I said, but I felt a wonderful light and joy coming into my soul, and I was beginning to see what the

Pharisees did not. Whether it was something in my words, or my manner, or my look, I know not: but all of a sudden a local preacher, who happened to be in the congregation, stood up, and putting up his arms, shouted out in Cornish manner, 'The parson is converted! the parson is converted! Hallelujah!' and in another moment his voice was lost in the shouts and praises of three or four hundred of the congregation. Instead of rebuking this extraordinary 'brawling,' as I should have done in a former time, I joined in the outburst of praise; and to make it more orderly, I gave out the Doxology—'Praise God, from whom all blessings flow'—and the people sang it with heart and voice, over and over again.

W. Haslam

O God my Father, life for that man born blind
would never be the same.
Unchanging darkness would become
light and colour, shade and shine, pattern and form,
meaning and vision and reality.
I do not wonder that he should say
'One thing I know...' when that
'one thing' should so transform his days!
And we in whose hearts by grace
your light has shined—
give us too that singleness of mind,
that all-embracing vision,
to know and care for one thing above all others—
the light of Christ.

A blind man given sight:
a lost man found: a man without Christ
converted by the Spirit's power.
Lord, I am all of these.
May that warmth and joy, that
transforming radiance of a totally new experience
not wholly fade. Just as your mercies
are new every morning,
so let my sense of them
be new as well.
Light out of darkness!
Life from the dead!
Christ in the heart!

Thank you, my Father, thank you,
from whom all blessings flow. Amen.

85

36. Faith in sorrow

When Martha heard that Jesus was coming, she went and met him, while Mary sat in the house. Martha said to Jesus, 'Lord, if you had been here, my brother would not have died. And even now I know that whatever you ask from God, God will give you.' Jesus said to her, 'Your brother will rise again.' Martha said to him, 'I know that he will rise again in the resurrection at the last day.' Jesus said to her, 'I am the resurrection and the life; he who believes in me, though he die, yet shall he live, and whoever lives and believes in me shall never die. Do you believe this?' She said to him, 'Yes, Lord; I believe that you are the Christ, the Son of God, he who is coming into the world.'

When she had said this, she went and called her sister Mary, saying quietly, 'The Teacher is here and is calling for you.' And when she heard it, she rose quickly and went to him. Now Jesus had not yet come to the village, but was still in the place where Martha had met him. When the Jews who were with her in the house, consoling her, saw Mary rise quickly and go out, they followed her, supposing that she was going to the tomb to weep there. Then Mary, when she came where Jesus was and saw him, fell at his feet, saying to him, 'Lord, if you had been here, my brother would not have died.' When Jesus saw her weeping, and the Jews who came with her also weeping, he was deeply moved in spirit and troubled; and he said 'Where have you laid him?' They said to him, 'Lord, come and see.' Jesus wept. So the Jews said, 'See how he loved him!' But some of them said, 'Could not he who opened the eyes of the blind man have kept this man from dying?'

John 11: 20–37

A few days ago I was talking to a young mother whom I have known for some years but had not met recently. She brought out a photograph of her three children to show me with a natural pride and joy, and spoke of them with evident happiness. Andrew, the middle one of the three, has recently left his family to go and live at home with the Lord, but his parents show no trace of resentment, or even of real grief. Right through this time of approaching loss and of actual bereavement, God has given them complete assurance that the boy was in His hands, and that all was well. Their triumph over a bitter sorrow has been a great testimony to God's loving dealings with them, a visible demonstration that His grace is sufficient for the deepest human need. I have written of this family, with their permission, because they point so clearly to the fact that it is not necessary to be stricken down by grief in personal bereavement, nor to question whether God cares. . . .

Both Martha and Mary, in the depths of their grief at their brother's death, said reproachfully to Jesus, 'If thou hadst been here, my brother had not died'. Jesus had been sent for during Lazarus' illness, and appeared to have delayed until too late. The sisters must have said to each other many times, in their mounting anxiety, 'If only Jesus were here'. They were to learn through their experience that Jesus was not only the healer, but the resurrection and the life, that death was power-

less before Him. But for us Christian families undergoing similar sorrow, there need never be any question of '*If thou hadst* been here.'
Helen Lee

How easy it is, O Lord my God,
to speak or write of
faith in sorrow,
strength in trial,
provided the sorrow and the trial are
someone else's!

Help me to grasp the faith and courage
of those sisters.
How sure they were of Christ!
How ready to see in him, whom
they so fully knew as man,
the resurrection and the life!
How strong to affirm that daring creed
'I believe
you are the Christ, the Son of God'!

And in this sorrow I see too, O Christ,
your sorrow:
your tears with theirs,
your love, a kind of loving
which, in a small way,
I can understand because I share.

One after another I hear those sisters say
'Lord, if you had been here ...'
What could have kept you?
Did you not know?
How could God let it happen?
Words like that I know that I shall never need to say.
Though I walk (as I expect to walk)
through the valley of the shadow of
death,
I will fear no evil for you are with me.
And you are Friend and Master and Shepherd,
and Resurrection and Life.

Therefore shall I lack nothing.
Thanks be to God. Amen.

37. Walking with Jesus

'Let not your hearts be troubled; believe in God, believe also in me. In my Father's house are many rooms; if it were not so, would I have told you that I go to prepare a place for you? And when I go and prepare a place for you, I will come again and will take you to myself, that where I am you may be also. And you know the way where I am going.' Thomas said to him, 'Lord, we do not know where you are going; how can we know the way?' Jesus said to him, 'I am the way, and the truth, and the life; no one comes to the Father, but by me. If you had known me, you would have known my Father also; henceforth you know him and have seen him.'

Philip said to him, 'Lord, show us the Father, and we shall be satisfied.' Jesus said to him, 'Have I been with you so long, and yet you do not know me, Philip? He who has seen me has seen the Father; how can you say, "Show us the Father?" Do you not believe that I am in the Father and the Father in me? The words that I say to you I do not speak on my own authority; but the Father who dwells in me does his works. Believe me that I am in the Father and the Father in me; or else believe me for the sake of the works themselves.'

John 14: 1–11

A more familiar relationship

I remember well a certain occasion, when I had already become a Christian. I believed in Jesus Christ, and loved Him. I took an active part in His Church, and communicated with Him at His Holy Table. But it was God, and not Jesus Christ, who occupied the centre of my devotional life. Of course, He is the same God; but in Jesus we see God more intimately and more nearly, 'being made in the likeness of men' (Philippians 2: 7). With Him there can be established a more familiar relationship than with the Father alone. There came a day when I was granted a vivid realization of this. I often used to visit, on Church business, an old pastor who never let me go without praying with me. He would address his prayers to Jesus, and I was struck one day by his extreme simplicity. It was as if he were continuing aloud an intimate conversation that he was always carrying on with Him.

When I got back home I talked it over with my wife, and together we asked God to give us also the close fellowship with Jesus that that old pastor had. Since then He has been the centre of my devotion and my travelling companion. He takes pleasure in what I do (cf. Ecclesiastes 9: 7), and concerns Himself with it. He is a friend with whom I can discuss everything that happens in my life. He shares my joy and my pain, my hopes and fears. He is there when a patient speaks to me from his heart, listening to him with me and better than I can. And when the patient has gone I can talk to Him about it.

This is no magical Utopia that I am describing. I know full well the dark places that remain, my own unfaithfulness in this continual trysting with Jesus. That is our human nature. Jesus Christ does not take our humanity from us; He comes down into it, so that I can bring my difficulties and failures to Him, and that also helps to maintain our fellowship.

Paul Tournier

Lord Jesus,
I too, like Philip,
have been with you a long time now.
I too, like that old pastor, or that doctor,
want to know a closer fellowship,
a more intimate trust.
And so I bring to you my
time of prayer.

Lord Jesus, I confess how little
appetite I seem to have sometimes
just to enjoy your friendship.
Oh, I turn soon enough
in trouble or indecision or
when I want something. And what
I want now
—or at least, I want to want it—
is to learn more of the open secret
shared by your deeper friends
—how to 'abide' within your love.
And so I bring this prayer to you,
beginning with today.
Restore my courage for that
difficult encounter. Quicken my sympathies
in the face of sorrow.
Open my eyes to see the beauty of your creation
and turn seeing into praise.
Release within me the springs of
thankfulness: stir my preoccupations to
unexpected joy. And keep my heart
turned towards you, Lord, just for this day
(tomorrow will take care of tomorrow)
as my Father's child
my Saviour's friend
a man in Christ.
For your Name's sake.
Amen.

38. Jesus of the scars

Now Thomas, one of the twelve, called the Twin, was not with them when Jesus came. So the other disciples told him, 'We have seen the Lord.' But he said to them, 'Unless I see in his hands the print of the nails, and place my finger in the mark of the nails, and place my hand in his side, I will not believe.'

Eight days later, his disciples were again in the house, and Thomas was with them. The doors were shut, but Jesus came and stood among them, and said, 'Peace be with you.' Then he said to Thomas, 'Put your finger here, and see my hands; and put out your hand, and place it in my side; do not be faithless, but believing.' Thomas answered him, 'My Lord and my God!' Jesus said to him, 'Have you believed because you have seen me? Blessed are those who have not seen and yet believe.'

John 20: 24–29

His credentials

To confirm their conviction that it is He Himself, *having said this he shewed both his hands and his side to them*. It was proof of identity; this, however transmuted, was the Body which had hung on the Cross and was laid in the tomb. But the scars are more than this; they are the evidence not only that what they see is the Body of Jesus, but what is the quality for ever of the Body of Him whom they know with ever-deeper understanding as the Christ: 'the Son of Man must suffer'.

The wounds of Christ are His credentials to the suffering race of men. Shortly after the end of the Great War, when its memories and its pains were fresh in mind, a volume was published under the title *Jesus of the Scars, and Other Poems* by Edward Shillito. The poem from which the title was taken stands first in the book and is headed by the text, 'He showed them His hands and His side':

If we have never sought, we seek Thee now;
    Thine eyes burn through the dark, our only stars;
We must have sight of thorn-pricks on Thy brow,
    We must have Thee, O Jesus of the Scars.

The heavens frighten us; they are too calm;
    In all the universe we have no place.
Our wounds are hurting us; where is the balm?
    Lord Jesus, by Thy Scars, we claim Thy grace.

If, when the doors are shut, Thou drawest near,
    Only reveal those hands, that side of Thine;
We know to-day what wounds are, have no fear,
    Show us Thy Scars, we know the countersign.

The other gods were strong; but Thou wast weak;
   They rode, but Thou didst stumble to a throne;
But to our wounds only God's wounds can speak,
   And not a god has wounds, but Thou alone.

Only a God in whose perfect Being pain has its place can win and
hold our worship; for otherwise the creature would in fortitude surpass
the Creator.

William Temple

Dear Lord,
I ponder that strange compulsion, which made you say
'The Son of Man must suffer'.
I suppose it was, partly at least, because you chose to be
the Son of Man.
Men suffer: and you chose to share our suffering.
   Men suffer, Lord, today and every day.
We know what it is to be hurt—badly hurt, sometimes—
in body, mind and spirit.
And away from our civilized, comfortable rut,
there are men and women
—yes, and children too—
with scars that they will never lose:
and pain of which they will never be free.
   And Lord, dimly I see, that as for Thomas, so for them,
no God or Lord or Saviour could be real
who knew their experience only in theory: and whose
effortless omnipotence
lifted him above their sufferings. They need, in fact,
a 'Jesus of the scars'.
And that is what they have!

O Lord, help me to feel and understand more deeply
the mysteries of suffering:
not that I dare to ask it,
except so far as it is within your will for me.
   So I pray now, not for myself (for I am in your hands)
but for sufferers without you:
who bear pain and loss and grief alone.
Give to your church a new compassion, a new sympathy
with all the dispossessed, the hurt, the scarred.
Help us to show to them a Saviour who bears the scars of love.

For your Name's sake. Amen.

39. The same person

After this Jesus revealed himself again to the disciples by the Sea of Tiberias; and he revealed himself in this way. Simon Peter, Thomas called the Twin, Nathanael of Cana in Galilee; the sons of Zebedee, and two others of his disciples were together. Simon Peter said to them, 'I am going fishing.' They said to him, 'We will go with you.' They went out and got into the boat; but that night they caught nothing.

Just as day was breaking, Jesus stood on the beach; yet the disciples did not know that it was Jesus. Jesus said to them, 'Children, have you any fish?' They answered him, 'No.' He said to them, 'Cast the net on the right side of the boat, and you will find some.' So they cast it, and now they were not able to haul it in, for the quantity of fish. That disciple whom Jesus loved said to Peter, 'It is the Lord!' When Simon Peter heard that it was the Lord, he put on his clothes, for he was stripped for work, and sprang into the sea. But the other disciples came in the boat, dragging the net full of fish, for they were not far from the land, but about a hundred yards off.

When they got out on land, they saw a charcoal fire there, with fish lying on it, and bread. Jesus said to them, 'Bring some of the fish that you have just caught.' So Simon Peter went aboard and hauled the net ashore, full of large fish, a hundred and fifty-three of them; and although there were so many, the net was not torn. Jesus said to them, 'Come and have breakfast.' Now none of the disciples dared ask him, 'Who are you?' They knew it was the Lord.

John 21: 1–12

Quite obviously Paul was right when he claimed that 'Christ being raised from the dead, will never die again; death has no longer dominion over him.' That in itself says something very remarkable about the body of Jesus after his resurrection. All human bodies are mortal. They lie under the 'dominion' of death. Or, to put it in more usual language, they begin to die from the moment they are born. But this new body of Jesus was not subject either to the sudden onslaught of disease or accident, nor to the insidious and irresistible process of growing old.

And this body was not confined within the limits of our space-time world. It simply could not have been composed as 'ordinary' bodies are. It may indeed have had 'flesh and bones', but it was not limited by them in the way we are. Bars and bolts could not shut it out, and death itself could not touch it. It was a *real* body, there can be no doubt about that. Hundreds of people could not have been so mistaken, especially when Jesus offered clear evidence of it. But it was not an earthbound body. It was something that bore a developmental relationship to an earthly human body, but it was not identical with it. There was clearly a continuity of life between the body of Jesus and the body of the resurrected Jesus, but in the process of resurrection it had undergone a very fundamental change. That, at least, seems obvious.

So much for the list of dissimilarities: the body of Jesus after the resurrection had a different appearance and also a different 'form'. It was 'like' the previous body, it had some sort of developmental relationship to it, but it was obviously not 'identical' with it.

Now we must consider the similarities. Strangely they all came down to one factor, but that factor is so important that it outweighs all the dissimilarities. It is simply this: Jesus before and after the resurrection was undeniably *the same person*. No matter what extraordinary changes had taken place in his bodily form, all who knew him well had no doubt at all who he was. They 'knew' it was the Lord.

David Winter

My Lord, what a morning!

The sun-rising and the world new-made:
that mysterious feeling of a dawn which follows
a night not spent in bed:
a deserted beach,
the colours returning as the mists disperse;
the first faint warmth, the extended shadows
of the early sun.
And Jesus there—different, of course, but
the same person.
      Recognized—and yet not wholly familiar,
moving among them in a resurrection body,
a foretaste of the new creation,
that world breaking into ours.
A kind of space-fiction situation
—or I should say, space-fact.

      And I shall meet you, Lord,
because of what you are,
in spite of what
I am.
May all our meeting and talking now
prepare me for
that day when it will truly be
'My Lord, what a morning!'
in resurrection life.

And may the glow of *that* morning, Lord,
be over *this* morning
and this day's work.

Amen.

40. Trial

Now when they heard these things they were enraged, and they ground their teeth against him. But he, full of the Holy Spirit, gazed into heaven and saw the glory of God, and Jesus standing at the right hand of God; and he said, 'Behold, I see the heavens opened, and the Son of man standing at the right hand of God.' But they cried out with a loud voice and stopped their ears and rushed together upon him. Then they cast him out of the city and stoned him; and the witnesses laid down their garments at the feet of a young man named Saul. And as they were stoning Stephen, he prayed, 'Lord Jesus, receive my spirit.' And he knelt down and cried with a loud voice, 'Lord, do not hold this sin against them.' And when he had said this, he fell asleep.

Acts 7: 54–60

Thomas Cranmer before his execution

And if he knew that the stake was to be set up in the morning, how did he spend that last night of trial and sorrow? We do not know. But we almost feel the throb of pain in that last lonely vigil, with its tears and shame, the shadow of failure, the trouble of conscience, and the longing for peace. Perhaps he would pour out his heart in the plaintive strains of his own beautiful Litany. Do we see that slender figure kneeling in the soft light of the candles, and can we hear his voice as it rehearsed those matchless words: 'That it may please Thee to bring into the way of truth all such as have erred, and are deceived: That it may please Thee to strengthen such as do stand; and to comfort and help the weak-hearted; and to raise up them that fall; and finally to beat down Satan under our feet: That it may please Thee to succour, help, and comfort all that are in danger, necessity, and tribulation: That it may please Thee to forgive our enemies, persecutors, and slanderers, and to turn their hearts: That it may please Thee to give us true repentance; to forgive us all our sins, negligences, and ignorances; and to endue us with the grace of Thy Holy Spirit to amend our lives according to Thy Holy Word.' He was still deep in the valley of doubts and fears, but there was a glimmer of light at last; and so into his very soul there came the Grace of God, and out of weakness he was made strong.

Marcus Loane

My Father,
I see again in this morning's paper
that torture is gaining ground as an
instrument of policy.

I pray for those who are facing trial,
suffering interrogation,
for no genuine crime. I pray for those
who are under terror, near to torture,
shrinking and afraid.

I pray for them.
I lift them to your care.
This man, here in this darkened cell—
this woman, and this, and this.
        You know them, Lord. Be near them.
Strengthen them. Sustain them, see them through.
And those who suffer for your sake, and for your Name,
grant them the heavens opened, the vision of glory,
faithful unto death.

And if that day should ever come for me—
not quite so impossible as once I thought—
then give me strength, carry me on your shoulders,
do for me what I could never do alone.
        I'm not the stuff
—even to say it is a sick joke—
I'm not the stuff that martyrs are made of.
So let me go on praying.
Let me walk close with Jesus now,
work where I can for justice in this world,
and leave my future in your hands.

Amen.

41. Out of prison

Herod the king laid violent hands upon some who belonged to the church.... He proceeded to arrest Peter also.... And when he had seized him, he put him in prison, and delivered him to four squads of soldiers to guard him, intending after the Passover to bring him out to the people. So Peter was kept in prison; but earnest prayer for him was made to God by the church.

The very night when Herod was about to bring him out, Peter was sleeping between two soldiers, bound with two chains, and sentries before the door were guarding the prison; and behold, an angel of the Lord appeared, and a light shone in the cell; and he struck Peter on the side and woke him, saying, 'Get up quickly.' And the chains fell off his hands. And the angel said to him, 'Dress yourself and put on your sandals.' And he did so. And he said to him, 'Wrap your mantle around you and follow me.' And he went out and followed him; he did not know that what was done by the angel was real, but thought he was seeing a vision. When they had passed the first and the second guard, they came to the iron gate leading into the city. It opened to them of its own accord, and they went out and passed on through one street; and immediately the angel left him. And Peter came to himself, and said, 'Now I am sure that the Lord has sent his angel and rescued me from the hand of Herod and from all that the Jewish people were expecting.'

When he realised this, he went to the house of Mary, the mother of John whose other name was Mark, where many were gathered together and were praying. And when he knocked at the door of the gateway, a maid named Rhoda came to answer. Recognising Peter's voice, in her joy she did not open the gate but ran in and told that Peter was standing at the gate. They said to her, 'You are mad.' But she insisted that it was so. They said, 'It is his angel!' But Peter continued knocking; and when they opened, they saw him and were amazed. But motioning to them with his hand to be silent, he described to them how the Lord had brought him out of the prison.

Acts 12: 1, 3–17

There is no human glory in intercessory prayer. The popular preacher may have his admiring crowd. He stands in a pulpit, 'high and lifted up.' The able evangelist, organiser, administrator, reformer and social-worker all move in a circle of those who know their fame and may envy their skill. But the intercessor (though he be more mighty than all the rest put together) receives no human admiration or applause. Those who benefit most by his titanic toil are often quite unaware of the channel of their bounty. He works in secret and his enormous service to the community is known only to God.

Friends may collect his letters after his death (as did the friends of Forbes Robinson) and the secret will be out. Or people will heap together their recollections of such a man and publish a memoir (as they did of Praying Hyde). But it is all posthumous. They have prayed in secret and God heard them in secret. The 'open' rewards which Jesus promised to the secret intercessors are not rewards which the world would heed. Their great reward is that they have more of the mind of Christ. It came almost as a by-product. They were not consciously seeking love, joy, peace, patience, ... they were seeking a blessing for someone else—a stranger maybe. Intercession became the important business of every day with them. Spending the secret hours asking a blessing for others, they open themselves to the greatest blessing of all. Christ comes and lives in them.

W. E. Sangster

O Lord, I laugh a little at this startled
prayer-meeting:
'Peter? *Peter outside?* Child,
you must be mad!'
    Is this the faith that believed you would hear
and answer prayer?

    And is mine so different?
    That prison stands for many situations,
many lives: Peter is the image of many in chains.
And for some of these I pray. I intercede. I ask—
I ask you, my divine Lord and Master,
to intervene.

And what do I expect to happen?
O God, I don't know that I want to answer that.

But it did happen! Whatever the failure of their expectations:
however earthbound their imaginings,
they went on praying.
    They prayed for Peter as he slept.
    They prayed, all unknowing, as he woke.
    They prayed on, blindly
as that iron gate swung open on to freedom.
And when Peter knocked at Mary's door
the church was praying still.

And you heard, you answered,
because you called them to pray.

So call me, Lord, to pray for others
and to go on praying.
Lord, give me faith, and keep me at it—
for your sake. Amen.

42. A reduced reality

For the wrath of God is revealed from heaven against all ungodliness and wickedness of men who by their wickedness suppress the truth. For what can be known about God is plain to them, because God has shown it to them. Ever since the creation of the world his invisible nature, namely, his eternal power and deity, has been clearly perceived in the things that have been made. So they are without excuse; for although they knew God they did not honour him as God or give thanks to him, but they became futile in their thinking and their senseless minds were darkened. Claiming to be wise, they became fools, and exchanged the glory of the immortal God for images resembling mortal man or birds or animals or reptiles.

Therefore God gave them up in the lusts of their hearts to impurity, to the dishonouring of their bodies among themselves, because they exchanged the truth about God for a lie and worshipped and served the creature rather than the Creator, who is blessed for ever! Amen.

For this reason God gave them up to dishonourable passions. Their women exchanged natural relations for unnatural, and the men likewise gave up natural relations with women and were consumed with passion for one another, men committing shameless acts with men and receiving in their own persons the due penalty for their error.

And since they did not see fit to acknowledge God, God gave them up to a base mind and to improper conduct. They were filled with all manner of wickedness, evil, covetousness, malice. Full of envy, murder, strife, deceit, malignity, they are gossips, slanderers, haters of God, insolent, haughty, boastful, inventors of evil, disobedient to parents, foolish, faithless, heartless, ruthless. Though they know God's decree that those who do such things deserve to die, they not only do them but approve those who practise them.

Romans 1: 18–32

Diderot wrote in the famous *Encylopedia* (1752–72) under the entry 'Man' that he 'seems to stand above the other animals'.... Man is really only an animal—who can *see* any basic difference? If we read on, and appreciate the spirit in which sentences like these were written, it comes down to this: there is no basic difference between man, animals, plants and things....

So man became 'natural', and lost his particular place in the cosmos. He lost his humanity. What does that mean? If man is just another animal, for instance, then what is 'love'? After a long development the answer came out loud and clear: Libido. Lust. Love is *really* only sex. All that seems to be more is 'in fact' sublimation, a nice kind of façade to hide the real drives. Sex one can see and experience. But love?

We must always be on our guard when we hear the word 'really' used like this. More often than not it means that an essential quality is removed! For the new science, which we should call mechanistic science, became a kind of 'revelation', the only way to get true knowledge. All things are *really* only natural things, animals, plants, non-living matter. There are no basic differences to the scientific eye. Science has become the revelation of the new world, and man clings superstitiously to the word scientific as true to reality. But it is a reduced reality.

The nineteenth century—and ours too—has laboured to work the new principles out. The result has been a *démasqué* in which many things held sacred or deep are brought down to what they *really* are: sex, lust, power, the survival of the fittest, an instinct or will to live. Life itself, instead of the varied and deep meaning it had in biblical language—man's full being, his true humanity, his work, dreams and aims, so that Christ Himself was able to say that He is the Life—life became nothing more than biological life, the beating heart and sexual urges and quest for food and drink. We can understand the man who, standing at the end of this development, asked recently in one of the underground papers, 'Is there a life before death?'

H. R. Rookmaaker

Thank you, my Father, that you are not a God who hides himself,
that you make yourself known
to honest searchers and open hearts.
    Help me, too, to learn the lesson
of the fragility of truth—
how readily corrupted, and how quickly lost.
How easy it is, my Father,
to turn the Truth of God into a lie!
To make the mind which you conceived as true
into a distorting mirror
      twisted by fallen nature,
      fogged by self-love,
      coloured by wishful thinking
so that in the end
'I ought' is nothing, and
'I want' is absolute.

And I see, my Father, even in my own experience
what a slippery slope this is.
Once I have blurred the lens of my mental spectacles
I cannot be sure that I can see to clean them.
So let me prize and value truth.
    And for what he is
let me prize and value man
to whom your truth is shown;
and for whom Christ himself
is Truth and Life.
Amen.

43. The law of the Spirit of life

There is therefore now no condemnation for those who are in Christ Jesus. For the law of the Spirit of life in Christ Jesus has set me free from the law of sin and death. For God has done what the law, weakened by the flesh, could not do: sending his own Son in the likeness of sinful flesh and for sin, he condemned sin in the flesh, in order that the just requirement of the law might be fulfilled in us, who walk not according to the flesh but according to the Spirit. For those who live according to the flesh set their minds on the things of the flesh, but those who live according to the Spirit set their minds on the things of the Spirit. To set the mind on the flesh is death, but to set the mind on the Spirit is life and peace. For the mind that is set on the flesh is hostile to God; it does not submit to God's law, indeed it cannot; and those who are in the flesh cannot please God.

But you are not in the flesh, you are in the Spirit, if the Spirit of God really dwells in you. Any one who does not have the Spirit of Christ does not belong to him. But if Christ is in you, although your bodies are dead because of sin, your spirits are alive because of righteousness. If the Spirit of him who raised Jesus from the dead dwells in you, he who raised Christ Jesus from the dead will give life to your mortal bodies also through his Spirit which dwells in you.

Romans 8: 1–11

Has this resurrection power, then, been withdrawn? Surely we are sent to proclaim that in Christ it is available still. And to the man who objects—'This power you talk of is not for me! I am not the stuff out of which God's Easter victories are made. Don't mock me with the mirage of Christlikeness. I know myself too well: my thwarting frailties are too baffling, the contradiction of my nature too inexorable, the chains of defeat too firmly shackled on my soul'—the real New Testament answer is to say: 'You surely do not imagine that the power which took Christ out of the grave is going to be baffled by you? That the God who did that colossal, prodigious act of might is going to find your problem too hard for His resources? That He who on that great day broke the last darkness of the universe may have to confess Himself impotent on the scale of your life and say, "I can achieve nothing here: this is too intractable for Me"? But that does not make sense,' these men of the New Testament protest, 'that doubt is utterly irrational! He who brought again from the dead the Lord Jesus, shall He not—to-day if you will ask Him—revive and quicken you?'

'Not for a moment,' exclaims Karl Barth, 'do we forget that our whole being and all our thoughts, words, and works are liable to utter damnation. But we ask: "Who is He that shall condemn? It is Christ that died, yea rather, that is risen again." It is because He is risen again ... that we put that question so defiantly. With that question we are merely allowing God to be God!'

J. S. Stewart

100

It rests in me, then, O my Father,
to set my mind where I would have it be.
Oh, I know that without help, I am not
even free to choose: the gravitational pull of evil
makes sure of that.
But equally, without my will,
even your power is fettered.
But that is because you choose, for my freedom's sake,
to stay your hand.
When I choose—by the Spirit's aid—why, then I know
and trust that the resurrection power
flows through me today
and, as Paul says,
'my spirit is alive because of righteousness'.

And so I set my mind.

You know me, Father, better than I can hope
to know myself.
You know how often my mind
drifts back—how tiny things divert it to another goal.
So day by day, hour by hour, as often as needs be
I set my mind.

I set my mind on Jesus, risen with him to a new life.
I set my mind on the Spirit, and his life in me
—his life and peace.
And so I find your freedom
        freedom to do right
        freedom from 'the law of sin and death'
        freedom from myself.
And in this way, Lord, I go forward.
I am a learner still
but I go forward, with my mind set.

Thank you, my Father.
In Christ's Name.

Amen.

44. Life an enemy?

We know that in everything God works for good with those who love him, who are called according to his purpose. For those whom he foreknew he also predestined to be conformed to the image of his Son, in order that he might be the first-born among many brethren. And those whom he predestined he also called; and those whom he called he also justified; and those whom he justified he also glorified.

What then shall we say to this? If God is for us, who is against us? He who did not spare his own Son but gave him up for us all, will he not also give us all things with him? Who shall bring any charge against God's elect? It is God who justifies: who is to condemn? Is it Christ Jesus, who died, yes, who was raised from the dead, who is at the right hand of God, who indeed intercedes for us? Who shall separate us from the love of Christ? Shall tribulation, or distress, or persecution, or famine, or nakedness, or peril, or sword? As it is written,

'For thy sake we are being killed all the day long;
we are regarded as sheep to be slaughtered.'

No, in all these things we are more than conquerors through him who loved us. For I am sure that neither death, nor life, nor angels, nor principalities, nor things present, nor things to come, nor powers, nor height, nor depth, nor anything else in all creation, will be able to separate us from the love of God in Christ Jesus our Lord.

Romans 8: 28–39

We have already seen that in Jesus we have seen the mind of God, and that mind is love. If then we say that the Word was active in creation it means that creation is the product of the mind of God which we see in Jesus Christ. This means that the same love which redeemed us created the world, that love is the principle of creation as love is the principle of redemption. There is a time in life when this may seem simply a theological or philosophical truth; but there is also a time in life when it is the only thing in life left to hold on to. There is a time when life and the world seem quite clearly to be an enemy, when life seems out to break our hearts, to ruin our dreams, and to smash our lives. There comes a time when we seem to be living in a hostile universe. At such a time it is the greatest thing in life, sometimes it is the only thing left, to be able to cling on to the conviction that 'life means intensely and it means good.' For if we believe that it was this mind of God in Jesus Christ which conceived and created the universe then it does mean that, whatever it feels like, God is working all things together for good, and the world is out not to break us but to make us. If the Christ of creation and the Christ of redemption are one and the same, then there is light even in the darkest hour.

Jesus is the Word. He is God's ultimate and final communication to men; he is the demonstration to men of the mind of God towards them; he is the guarantee that at the heart of creation there is love.

William Barclay

102

O God, my Father
how easy it is to believe and to rejoice
when all goes well! But there come times
when life does seem to be an enemy.
I think, my Father, that I have only touched
the edges of this dark experience. But there
is plenty of testimony from those who know it well,
     in deep intensity
      in unremitting darkness
       over a long time continuously.
I pray for them. I intercede for those 'who sit in darkness';
especially where their focus is unrelieved by any
kindly light of reason.

Especially for him ... and him ... and her.
And as I pray for them, I reaffirm before you
my faith that it is
your goodness
on which our universe is founded,
on which our life is built.
I thank you, my God, that what I see of you in Christ,
and of your love in the redemption that he won,
I believe of you in all creation; even, sometimes,
in spite of its appearances.
     So when the dark day comes, keep me in this faith.
I dare not pray that it *will* come. I pray as Jesus taught us,
    'Lead us not into temptation
     but deliver us from evil.'
But if it should, help me to stand: to be
'more than conqueror'.
And in my petty moments of gloom, depression, irritation,
self-pity,
help me to fix my eyes upon your love.
Through Jesus Christ our Lord.

Amen.

45. Enough to live for

For Christ did not send me to baptize but to preach the gospel, and not with eloquent wisdom, lest the cross of Christ be emptied of its power.

For the word of the cross is folly to those who are perishing, but to us who are being saved it is the power of God. For it is written,

'I will destroy the wisdom of the wise,

and the cleverness of the clever I will thwart.'

Where is the wise man? Where is the scribe? Where is the debater of this age? Has not God made foolish the wisdom of the world? For since, in the wisdom of God, the world did not know God through wisdom, it pleased God through the folly of what we preach to save those who believe. For Jews demand signs and Greeks seek wisdom, but we preach Christ crucified, a stumbling block to Jews and folly to Gentiles, but to those who are called, both Jews and Greeks, Christ the power of God and the wisdom of God. For the foolishness of God is wiser than men, and the weakness of God is stronger than men.

1 Corinthians 1: 17–25

The last night of D. L. Moody's mission in Cambridge, 1882

After repeating the warning, 'Jesus Christ said, "if you believe not, ye shall die in your sins: whither I go ye cannot come," ' Moody said: 'One last word. I've enjoyed preaching to you students as much as anything I have ever done in my life. I shall never forget this week, though you may forget me. I thank God I ever came to Cambridge, but I should like to give you one text before closing. "Seek ye *first* the kingdom of God." ' He told them another story to illustrate the dangers of delay, reminded them that they were starting life and their characters were forming, and ended with the words, 'Believe the Gospel and make room for God in your hearts.'

After the choir had sung 'Just as I am, without one plea,' Moody led in prayer, while all knelt or sat. Then he asked that those who had received blessing during the week should rise quietly in their places, silent prayer continuing and all eyes closed. And Moule, kneeling next to Moody on the platform heard him say under his breath as he looked up and saw some two hundred on their feet: 'My God, this is enough to live for.'

J. C. Pollock

Enough to live for?

What do I live for now, my God and Father?
'Seek first the kingdom of God,' said Jésus.
      What am I seeking first?
'Make room for God in your hearts,' said Moody
to those men at Cambridge:
Two hundred on their feet!
This was his calling and his ministry.

      What about me?
O God, for Christ and for his cross,
      for the power of that cross,
      for the Word of the cross
      for Jesus Christ,
      the divine wisdom and the divine word,
      stronger than self and sin
      wiser than intellect or fear or doubt,
I thank you.

Help me enlarge the room I give you in my heart:
day following day, by filling my life more.
      Teach me to work for Jesus and his kingdom
which will make me say, even though no-one
hears it but you and me,
'My God, this is enough to live for.'

Amen.

46. For the sake of the gospel

Do you not know that those who are employed in the temple service get their food from the temple, and those who serve at the altar share in the sacrificial offerings? In the same way, the Lord commanded that those who proclaim the gospel should get their living by the gospel.

But I have made no use of any of these rights, nor am I writing this to secure any such provision. For I would rather die than have any one deprive me of my ground for boasting. For if I preach the gospel, that gives me no ground for boasting. For necessity is laid upon me. Woe to me if I do not preach the gospel! For if I do this of my own will, I have a reward; but if not of my own will, I am entrusted with a commission. What then is my reward? Just this; that in my preaching I may make the gospel free of charge, not making full use of my right in the gospel....

Do you not know that in a race all the runners compete, but only one receives the prize? So run that you may obtain it. Every athlete exercises self-control in all things. They do it to receive a perishable wreath, but we an imperishable. Well, I do not run aimlessly. I do not box as one beating the air; but I pommel my body and subdue it, lest after preaching to others I myself should be disqualified.

1 Corinthians 9: 13–18, 24–27

Hudson Taylor, aged 19, writes home from Hull, 1852

As to my health, I think I never was so well and hearty in my life. The winds here are extremely searching, but as I always wrap up well I am pretty secure.... The cold weather gives me a good appetite, and it would be dear economy to stint myself. So I take as much plain, substantial food as I need, but waste nothing on luxuries. In going to my lodgings I have somehow got into one particular route, and always go the same way and cross at the same place. I have never passed the gate once, and at night the reflection of the lamps and windows opposite are always shining on the Drain.

I have found some brown biscuits which are really as cheap as bread, eighteen pence a stone, and much nicer. For breakfast I have biscuit and herring, which is cheaper than butter (three for a penny, and half a one is enough) with coffee. For dinner I have at present a prune-and-apple pie. Prunes are two or three pence a pound and apples tenpence a peck. I use no sugar but loaf, which I powder, and at fourpence halfpenny a pound I find it is cheaper than the coarser kind. Sometimes I have roast potatoes and tongue, which is as inexpensive as any other meat. For tea I have biscuit and apples. I take no supper, or occasionally a little biscuit and apple. Sometimes I have a rice pudding, a few peas boiled instead of potatoes, and now and then some fish. By being wide awake I can get cheese at fourpence to sixpence a pound that is better than we often have at home for eightpence. Now I see rhubarb and lettuce in the market, so I shall soon have another change. I pickled a penny red cabbage with three halfpence worth of vinegar, which made me a large jar full. So you see, at little expense I enjoy

106

many comforts. To these add a home where every want is anticipated, and 'the peace of God which passeth all understanding,' and if I were not happy and contented I should deserve to be miserable.

Quoted by Dr and Mrs Howard Taylor

For all links in the chain,
O Lord my God,
that brought to me the story of the gospel—
    I thank you, Father, with all my heart.

For Christ himself, author
and finisher
of our faith;
for Christ who is himself the
good news for all mankind—
    I thank you, Father, with all my heart.

For saints and martyrs, teachers
and evangelists; for that
apostolic company; and for Paul,
'unfit to be called an apostle'
whose words I read today—
    I thank you, Father, with all my heart.

And so it goes on; and always at
a price.
in toil and labour, in pain and blood,
the good news spreads from place to place,
generation to generation.
For all who shared in the
missionary task—
    I thank you, Father, with all my heart.

And for my chance to be
myself a link in this great chain,
a bearer of good news of Christ
to other men,
    I thank you, Father, with all my heart.

And may it be a heart of love,
of joy and praise!
For Jesus' sake. Amen.

47. A deeper country; a sunlit land

But someone will ask, 'How are the dead raised? With what kind of body do they come?' You foolish man! What you sow does not come to life unless it dies. And what you sow is not the body which is to be, but a bare kernel, perhaps of wheat or of some other grain. But God gives it a body as he has chosen, and to each kind of seed its own body....

So is it with the resurrection of the dead. What is sown is perishable, what is raised is imperishable. It is sown in dishonour, it is raised in glory. It is sown in weakness, it is raised in power. It is sown a physical body, it is raised a spiritual body. If there is a physical body, there is also a spiritual body. Thus it is written, 'The first man Adam became a living being'; the last Adam became a life-giving spirit. But it is not the spiritual which is first but the physical, and then the spiritual.

The first man was from the earth, a man of dust; the second man is from heaven. As was the man of dust, so are those who are of the dust; and as is the man of heaven, so are those who are of heaven. Just as we have borne the image of the man of dust, we shall also bear the image of the man of heaven. I tell you this, brethren: flesh and blood cannot inherit the kingdom of God, nor does the perishable inherit the imperishable.

1 Corinthians 15:35–38, 42–50

The real Narnia

'The Eagle is right,' said the Lord Digory. 'Listen, Peter. When Aslan said you could never go back to Narnia, he meant the Narnia you were thinking of. But that was not the real Narnia. That had a beginning and an end. It was only a shadow or a copy of the real Narnia which has always been here and always will be here: just as our own world, England and all, is only a shadow or copy of something in Aslan's real world. You need not mourn over Narnia, Lucy. All of the old Narnia that mattered, all the dear creatures, have been drawn into the real Narnia through the Door. And of course it is different; as different as a real thing is from a shadow or as waking life is from a dream.' ...

It is as hard to explain how this sunlit land was different from the old Narnia as it would be to tell you how the fruits of that country taste. Perhaps you will get some idea of it if you think like this. You may have been in a room in which there was a window that looked out on a lovely bay of the sea or a green valley that wound away among mountains. And in the wall of that room opposite to the window there may have been a looking-glass. And as you turned away from the window you suddenly caught sight of that sea or that valley, all over again, in the looking-glass. And the sea in the mirror, or the valley in the mirror, were in one sense just the same as the real ones: yet at the same time they were somehow different—deeper, more wonderful, more like places in a story: in a story you have never heard but very much want to know. The difference between the old Narnia and the new Narnia was like that. The new one was a deeper country: every rock and flower and blade of grass looked as if it meant more. I can't describe it any better than that: if ever you get there you will know what I mean.

C. S. Lewis

Lord, let me not be afraid of growing old.
You know (who better?) that old age
terrifies
one sometimes.
I see this body, this flesh and blood,
ageing, succumbing, failing even.
Day by day my body begins to remind me—
well, month by month, anyway—that it is
perishable stuff.
And this, my Father, is part of your purpose now.
Flesh and blood cannot inherit the kingdom of God.

In that deeper country,
that real and sunlit land of which ours is
      a reflection,
      a shadow,
what is sown in weakness here, perishable, common, earthly,
impermanent,
is raised imperishable, spiritual, eternal
in glory and power.
All of this world that matters then
will be with us still
'drawn in through the Door'.
I shall not grieve for youth, or friends,
or loss, or weakness, or past loves.
The Man of Heaven—you, Lord—
will be there. Your image
will be mine.
The dream will be over.
When I wake up after your likeness
I shall be satisfied with it.

So let me live this day as one
on pilgrimage
who seeks a better country, that is, a heavenly.

Amen.

48. Better things ahead

Lo! I tell you a mystery. We shall not all sleep, but we shall all be changed, in a moment, in the twinkling of an eye, at the last trumpet. For the trumpet will sound, and the dead will be raised imperishable, and we shall be changed. For this perishable nature must put on the imperishable, and this mortal nature must put on immortality. When the perishable puts on the imperishable, and the mortal puts on immortality, then shall come to pass the saying that is written:

'Death is swallowed up in victory.'
'O death, where is thy victory?
O death, where is thy sting?'
The sting of death is sin, and the power of sin is the law. But thanks be to God, who gives us the victory through our Lord Jesus Christ.

Therefore, my beloved brethren, be steadfast, immovable, always abounding in the work of the Lord, knowing that in the Lord your labour is not in vain.

1 Corinthians 15:51–58

Magdalene College,
Cambridge
17 June 63

Dear Mary

This is terrible news. The doctor who refused to come would, I think, be liable to criminal prosecution in this country.

Pain is terrible, but surely you need not have fear as well? Can you not see death as the friend and deliverer? It means stripping off that body which is tormenting you; like taking off a hairshirt or getting out of a dungeon. What is there to be afraid of? You have long attempted (and none of us does more) a Christian life. Your sins are confessed and absolved. Has this world been so kind to you that you should leave it with regret? There are better things ahead than any we leave behind.

Remember, tho' we struggle against things because we are afraid of them, it is often the other way round—we get afraid *because* we struggle. Are you struggling, resisting? Don't you think Our Lord says to you 'Peace, child, peace. Relax. Let go. Underneath are the everlasting arms. Let go, I will catch you. Do you trust me so little?'

Of course this may not be the end. Then make it a good rehearsal.

Yours (and like you a tired traveller,
near the journey's end)
Jack

C. S. Lewis

110

We don't talk much about death today, Lord;
it might be better if we did.
        I imagine I'm not alone
in thinking about it from time to time.
Like many things, it's easier to think about calmly
the further away it seems to be.
But none of us is ever very far away
from the immediate *possibility* of death—
one breath away, perhaps. The thought
adds a new value to the assurance
of forgiveness.

Through you, Lord Christ, the sting of death is drawn;
you tasted death
for every man.
Because of that—only because of that—can we recall
that underneath
are the everlasting arms.
Peace, then, my Lord—your peace for me.
And through me, I dare to ask, your peace
for others.

The lesson of inevitable death seems to be
steadfastness, confidence;
unshakable, immovable;
and to do my work of today.
        'A Christian life', Jack writes to Mary:
'You have long attempted a Christian life.'
O Lord, you know the value of my small attempts.
Let me not rest in them, only in you.
Yours is the victory, and therefore
mine.
And my danger, Lord, is that though I do believe
there are better things ahead,
yet I love life. The world *is* kind to me:
shall I fear death more and more as the years pass?
I pray not.
Let me let go. I trust you, for death, Lord,
and for life.

Amen.

49. On behalf of Christ

Therefore, if any one is in Christ, he is a new creation; the old has passed away, behold, the new has come. All this is from God, who through Christ reconciled us to himself and gave us the ministry of reconciliation; that is, God was in Christ reconciling the world to himself, not counting their trespasses against them, and entrusting to us the message of reconciliation. So we are ambassadors for Christ, God making his appeal through us. We beseech you on behalf of Christ, be reconciled to God. . . .

We put no obstacle in any one's way, so that no fault may be found with our ministry, but as servants of God we commend ourselves in every way: through great endurance, in afflictions, hardships, calamities, beatings, imprisonments, tumults, labours, watching, hunger; by purity, knowledge, forbearance, kindness, the Holy Spirit, genuine love, truthful speech, and the power of God; with the weapons of righteousness for the right hand and for the left; in honour and dishonour, in ill repute and good repute. We are treated as impostors, and yet are true; as unknown, and yet well known; as dying, and behold we live; as punished, and yet not killed; as sorrowful, yet always rejoicing; as poor, yet making many rich; as having nothing, and yet possessing everything.

2 Corinthians 5: 17–20; 6: 3–10

An ideal of sacred ministry

Christian saw the picture of a very grave person hang up against the wall; and this was the fashion of it. It had eyes lifted up to heaven, the best of books in his hand, the law of truth was written upon his lips, the world was behind his back. It stood as if it pleaded with men, and a crown of gold did hang over his head.

Then said Christian, What meaneth this?

The man whose picture this is, is one of a thousand, he can beget children (1 Corinthians 4: 15), travail in birth with children (Galatians 4: 19), and nurse them himself when they are born. And whereas thou seest him with his eyes lift up to heaven, the best of books in his hand, and the law of truth writ on his lips, it is to show thee that his work is to know and unfold dark things to sinners; even as also thou seest him stand as if he pleaded with men; and whereas thou seest the world as cast behind him, and that a crown hangs over his head, that is to show thee that slighting and despising the things that are present, for the love that he hath to his Master's service, he is sure in the world that comes next to have glory for his reward. Now, said the Interpreter, I have showed thee this picture first, because the man whose picture this is, is the only man whom the Lord of the place whither thou art going, hath authorised to be thy guide in all difficult places thou mayest meet with in the way; wherefore, take good heed to what I have showed thee, and bear well in thy mind what thou hast seen, lest in thy journey thou meet with some that pretend to lead thee right, but their way goes down to death.

John Bunyan

112

I tremble, God:
and it's enough to make anyone tremble—
let alone a minister of Christ's gospel.

As I read these extracts—by brave
men who knew prison from the inside—
these great ideals fall like the blows of a hammer:
what does Paul say?
　　　'gave us the ministry—
　　　ambassadors for Christ—
　　　God making his appeal through us—
　　　we beseech you on behalf of Christ—
　　　working together with him—'
and then the great lists of endurance and affliction
of the fruits of the Spirit
of the paradox of ministry.

　　　Lord, who is sufficient for these things? Alas, not I!
How many of us, Lord, are children of our time
in the work of the ministry, not firmly rooted
in the timeless heart of our calling?
But when you call, you equip:
and so I pray
for all Christian workers,
missionaries, ministers, pastors,
teachers, shepherds,
and especially for these my friends, by name.

　　　Keep clear in all of us the vision of
your priorities.
Give us the humility that belongs to servants,
and the authority
that belongs to servants of a great Master.
Give us high ideals, and the
Spirit's strength to reach them, and to raise them,
even in our middle age!
For the sake of Jesus, your Son, our Lord
who calls us to his service.
Amen.

50. Liberty!

For freedom Christ has set us free; stand fast therefore, and do not submit again to a yoke of slavery....

For you were called to freedom, brethren; only do not use your freedom as an opportunity for the flesh, but through love be servants of one another. For the whole law is fulfilled in one word, 'You shall love your neighbour as yourself.' But if you bite and devour one another take heed that you are not consumed by one another.

But I say, walk by the Spirit, and do not gratify the desires of the flesh. For the desires of the flesh are against the Spirit, and the desires of the Spirit are against the flesh; for these are opposed to each other, to prevent you from doing what you would. But if you are led by the Spirit you are not under the law. Now the works of the flesh are plain: immorality, impurity, licentiousness, idolatry, sorcery, enmity, strife, jealousy, anger, selfishness, dissension, party spirit, envy, drunkenness, carousing, and the like. I warn you, as I warned you before, that those who do such things shall not inherit the kingdom of God. But the fruit of the Spirit is love, joy, peace, patience, kindness, goodness, faithfulness, gentleness, self-control; against such there is no law. And those who belong to Christ Jesus have crucified the flesh with its passions and desires.

If we live by the Spirit, let us also walk by the Spirit. Let us have no self-conceit, no provoking of one another, no envy of one another.

Galatians 5. 1: 13–26

We must resist the ever-present temptation that, having become Christians through simple faith in Christ and all He has done for us, we now seek to maintain our Christian life by the keeping of moral laws. 'Through the Spirit', [Paul] continues, 'we wait for the hope of righteousness ... faith working through love.' This is the great law, the one law, for the Christian, the law of love, for 'love is the fulfilling of the law'. In saying this, however, he is saying something tremendous, because there is no such thing, correctly speaking, as free love. Love is the most binding force on earth.

Here is a daughter going to Canada, let us say, for a year. She and her mother are devoted to each other. From one point of view it would be much easier for the girl, perhaps, if her mother gave her a list of twenty rules to keep if she was to be a dutiful daughter, pleasing her mother. That would leave the girl quite free to do anything she liked outside the ground covered by the twenty rules. But love is more binding than that. The mother gives her no rules, yet in the girl's mind and heart there is a consciousness of what would please her mother and what would not. This knowledge is inconvenient, for it covers the whole of life, both the known and the unknown situations, both the present and the future. Because she loves her mother she will always find the challenge and standard for her actions. She lives under love, and not under law.

Bryan Green

Love, Joy, Peace!

A remote and sunlit valley, drowsy in the warmth of summer,
and a calm shining sea beyond.
      And yet, my Lord Jesus,
you did not live much of your life in
sheltered calm
withdrawn from a rougher, tougher
real world
outside. Your love and joy and peace
came from inside: not from circumstance.
      Whatever happened, sun or storm,
you were free.
And I am called to the same freedom,
led by your Spirit,
no more under law, because I belong to you—
called to the freedom that lies in
resurrection,
on the further side of
death.

So let me cherish freedom—
fighting to defend it against those temptations
that offer a yoke of bondage
however comfortable at first they seem.
And let my freedom express itself
not in law
—there are not laws of that sort in a world of liberty—
but in love.
And may the same Spirit,
your Holy Spirit,
add to love those other fruits from his sunlit orchard:
joy, peace, patience, kindness,
goodness, faithfulness, gentleness,
self-mastery
in Christ.

For his Name's sake.

Amen.

51. The gift of God

And you he made alive, when you were dead through the trespasses and sins in which you once walked, following the course of this world, following the prince of the power of the air, the spirit that is now at work in the sons of disobedience. Among these we all once lived in the passions of our flesh, following the desires of body and mind, and so we were by nature children of wrath, like the rest of mankind. But God, who is rich in mercy, out of the great love with which he loved us, even when we were dead through our trespasses, made us alive together with Christ (by grace you have been saved), and raised us up with him, and made us sit with him in the heavenly places in Christ Jesus, that in the coming ages he might show the immeasurable riches of his grace in kindness toward us in Christ Jesus. For by grace you have been saved through faith; and this is not your own doing, it is the gift of God–not because of works, lest any man should boast. For we are his workmanship, created in Christ Jesus for good works, which God prepared beforehand, that we should walk in them.

Ephesians 2: 1–10

On October 16, 1555, [Ridley] and Latimer were burnt at Oxford. In the long farewell which [Nicholas Ridley] wrote from prison while waiting for the end, there is a moving passage about his old College.

Farewell Pembroke Hall, of late mine own College, my Cure and my charge: what case thou art in now God knoweth, I know not well. Thou wast ever named since I knew thee, which is now thirty years ago, to be studious, well learned, and a great setter forth of Christ's gospel, and of God's true word; so I found thee, and blessed be God so I left thee indeed. Wo is mee for thee, my own dear College, if ever thou suffer thyself by any means to be brought from that trade. In thy Orchard (the walls, buts, and trees, if they could speake, would beare me witnesse) I learned without booke almost all Pauls Epistles, yea and I ween all the Canonicall Epistles, save only the Apocalypse. Of which studie although in time a great part did depart from me, yet the sweet smell thereof I trust I shall carry with me into heaven: for the profit thereof I think I have felt in all my lifetime ever after, and I ween of late (whether they abide now or no) there was that did the like. The Lord grant that this zeale and love toward that part of Gods word, which is a key and true commentary to all the holy Scriptures, may ever abide in that Colledge so long as the World shall endure.

Aubrey Attwater

Alive!
Alive with Christ!
Words fail me, Lord!

And yet I turn to words to make
my prayer. For you yourself,
my God and Lord,
give to us words, a Word, by which
to reach our spirits and our hearts.
How well your children know
that 'sweet smell' of Scripture studied
and absorbed
which speaks peace to the conscience,
        joy to the heart,
        life to the soul,
because it unfolds Christ's gospel
revealed
in God's true word.

My prayer, then, begins in
thankfulness. I thank you, Lord,
for your rich mercy, your great love,
the immeasurable riches of
your saving grace.
        I thank you for destiny,
the pre-ordaining of your perfect will.
        I thank you for life
out of death. I thank you above all
for Christ.

And my prayer concludes:
that zeal and love may continue
in me, and all your children,
        fed by your Word,
        resting in Christ,
        ready for the best—or worst—the future holds
of joy or pain, life or death,
because we are alive
for evermore.

Amen.

52. Intercessors

I thank my God in all my remembrance of you, always in every prayer of mine for you all making my prayer with joy, thankful for your partnership in the gospel from the first day until now. And I am sure that he who began a good work in you will bring it to completion at the day of Jesus Christ. It is right for me to feel thus about you all, because I hold you in my heart, for you are all partakers with me of grace, both in my imprisonment and in the defence and confirmation of the gospel. For God is my witness, how I yearn for you all with the affection of Christ Jesus. And it is my prayer that your love may abound more and more, with knowledge and all discernment, so that you may approve what is excellent, and may be pure and blameless for the day of Christ, filled with the fruits of righteousness which come through Jesus Christ, to the glory and praise of God.

Philippians 1: 3–11

Reflecting on what to ask

I am in the habit of preparing the substance of my private and family prayers. I believe that we are far too extempore in that duty; not that I recommend any verbal preparation, but a meditation upon the points on which we wish to ask the help of God. The want of this seems to me to lead the mind to wander about, and rather to fill our mouths with a train of words to which we are accustomed than our hearts with a sense of our necessities. I, at least, have found the habit of reflecting on what I shall ask for, before I venture to ask, highly serviceable.

I am bound to acknowledge that I have always found that my prayers have been heard and answered—not that I have in every instance (though in almost every instance I have) received what I asked for, nor do I expect or wish it. I always qualify my petitions by adding, provided that what I ask for is for my real good and according to the will of my Lord. But with this qualification I feel at liberty to submit my wants and wishes to God in small things as well as in great; and I am inclined to imagine that there are no 'little things' with Him. We see that His attention is as much bestowed upon what we call trifles, as upon those things which we consider of mighty importance. His hand is as manifest in the feathers of a butterfly's wing, in the eye of an insect, in the folding and packing of a blossom, in the curious aqueducts by which a leaf is nourished, as in the creation of a world and in the laws by which the planets move.

Thomas Fowell Buxton

Thank you, Lord, for intercessors—
for those who, when they have me or mine in mind,
bring us before you in their prayers
with joy.
Thank you for those who hold us in their hearts—
and hold us up before your face in prayer.

Teach me to use this gift of intercession
      to train myself in it
      to persevere
      to take it seriously.
Keep before me a sense of wonder that you who devised
'the laws by which the planets move'
can yet be interested—concerned—in our affairs.

So now I make a list:
      I pray for him, not far perhaps from the
        kingdom: may your Spirit strive with him today;
       for her, growing out of childhood, that she may
        grow up unto Christ in all things;
       for another, facing loneliness and the temptation
       to despair;
and many more! Perhaps, Lord, I would do best
to put them on another list—tomorrow's, and the day after,
and so remember them by name:
      a missionary far from home,
      a mother anxious for a child,
      a friend to whom I owe so much.
Lord, I intercede for them. Work in each one of them
the perfect pleasure of your will.

For Jesus Christ's sake.

Amen.

53. Fullness of deity

For I want you to know how greatly I strive for you, and for those at Laodicea, and for all who have not seen my face, that their hearts may be encouraged as they are knit together in love, to have all the riches of assured understanding and the knowledge of God's mystery, of Christ, in whom are hid all the treasures of wisdom and knowledge. I say this in order that no one may delude you with beguiling speech. For though I am absent in body, yet I am with you in spirit, rejoicing to see your good order and the firmness of your faith in Christ.

As therefore you received Christ Jesus the Lord, so live in him, rooted and built up in him and established in the faith, just as you were taught, abounding in thanksgiving.

See to it that no one makes a prey of you by philosophy and empty deceit, according to human tradition, according to the elemental spirits of the universe, and not according to Christ. For in him the whole fullness of deity dwells bodily, and you have come to fullness of life in him, who is the head of all rule and authority. In him also you were circumcised with a circumcision made without hands, by putting off the body of flesh in the circumcision of Christ; and you were buried with him in baptism, in which you were also raised with him through faith in the working of God, who raised him from the dead. And you, who were dead in trespasses and the uncircumcision of your flesh, God made alive together with him, having forgiven us all our trespasses, having cancelled the bond which stood against us with its legal demands; this he set aside, nailing it to the cross. He disarmed the principalities and powers and made a public example of them, triumphing over them in him.

Colossians 2: 1–15

Problems in Scripture

Someone brings us a problem, maybe an apparent discrepancy or a question of literary criticism. What shall we do? To begin with, we shall wrestle with the problem, and perhaps find fresh light on it. But we may well not entirely solve it. So then what? Must we abandon our belief in the Word of God until we have solved all the problems? No. We shall maintain our belief in God's Word, just as we maintain our belief in God's love, in spite of the problems, ultimately for one reason and for one reason only, namely that Jesus Christ taught it and exhibited it. It is no more obscurantist to cling to the one belief than the other. Indeed, it is not obscurantist at all. To follow Christ is always sober, humble, Christian realism.

... The ultimate issue in the question of authority concerns the lordship of Christ. 'You call Me Teacher and Lord', He said, 'and you are right; for so I am'. If Jesus Christ is truly our teacher and our lord, we are under both His instruction and His authority. We must therefore bring our mind into subjection to Him as our teacher and our will into subjection to Him as our lord. We have no liberty to disagree with Him or to disobey Him. So we bow to the authority of Scripture because we bow to the authority of Christ.

John Stott

O Christ, O Christ, O Christ.
How small my vision of you, Christ, my Lord!
In you, to whom I come with these poor
maunderings, in you
are hid the treasures of wisdom and knowledge.
    In you
the whole fulness of deity dwells.
    In you
have I been buried by baptism,
        And with you
raised, and made alive.

'Ransomed, healed, restored, forgiven,
who like me his praise should sing?'

O Christ, I take you for my wisdom and
my authority. I bring myself, yes, even
my wilful speculative mind,
into subjection to your teaching.
Sharpen this intellect you gave me,
enliven it, train it, help me to use it
—but with you as its Lord.
You know how I like to have my own way—
intellectually as well as practically. Help me
to make your way,
my way;
your will,
my will;
your written word my guide and rule, to which I bow;
O Christ, my teacher and my Lord.

Amen.

54. The living word of truth

You then, my son, be strong in the grace that is in Christ Jesus, and what you have heard from me before many witnesses entrust to faithful men who will be able to teach others also. Take your share of suffering as a good soldier of Christ Jesus. No soldier on service gets entangled in civilian pursuits, since his aim is to satisfy the one who enlisted him. An athlete is not crowned unless he competes according to the rules. It is the hard-working farmer who ought to have the first share of the crops. Think over what I say, for the Lord will grant you understanding in everything.

Remember Jesus Christ, risen from the dead, descended from David, as preached in my gospel, the gospel for which I am suffering and wearing fetters like a criminal. But the word of God is not fettered. Therefore I endure everything for the sake of the elect, that they also may obtain the salvation which in Christ Jesus goes with eternal glory. The saying is sure:
If we have died with him, we shall also live with him;
if we endure, we shall also reign with him;
if we deny him, he also will deny us;
if we are faithless, he remains faithful—
for he cannot deny himself.

Remind them of this, and charge them before the Lord to avoid disputing about words, which does no good, but only ruins the hearers. Do your best to present yourself to God as one approved, a workman who has no need to be ashamed, rightly handling the word of truth.

2 Timothy 2: 1–15

The New Testament Letters

It seems that the men who wrote these letters concentrated upon the essential spiritual core of human life. They provide that spiritual vitamin, without which human life is at best sickly, and at worst dead. While scarcely touching on any 'modern problem' they yet manage to give pointers of principle which show the way, and the spirit, in which the problems of even a highly complex age such as ours may be tackled successfully.

The present translator who has closely studied these letters for several years is struck by two things. First, their surprising vitality. Without holding fundamentalist views on 'inspiration', he is continually struck by the living quality of the material on which he is working. Some will, no doubt, consider it merely superstitious reverence for 'Holy Writ', yet again and again the writer felt rather like an electrician re-wiring an ancient house without being able to 'turn the mains off'. He feels that this fact is worth recording. Secondly, he is struck by the extraordinary unanimity of the letters. The cynic may suggest that these men were all in a conspiracy together (though it is difficult to see what motive they could have for such a thing), yet the fact remains that in their different ways and from their different angles they are all talking about the same thing, and talking with such certainty as to bring a wondering envy into the modern heart.

J. B. Phillips

122

Lord Jesus Christ
I do remember you, even as I talk with you now,
and all that I remember comes to me
from a single source—
the living word of truth, the holy
Scriptures:
words written down
to convey truth and life to those who come after.

I thank you, Lord, for those first
witnesses:
and for the faithful men who witnessed
in their turn
and suffered for it.
I thank you for the gospel of salvation
which comes to me,
and all today's world
as the good news of God.

So make me a better student of your Word:
a workman, labouring;
a tradesman, experienced;
a craftsman, skilled.
Make me a better listener to your Word;
a better discerner, and
a better witness too.

I know, Lord, that spiritual power
lies not in printed words
but in yourself, and in your
Holy Spirit. So may he
open to me
the truth I need to learn,
and touch with power
my springs of thought and action.
For your Name's sake.

Amen.

55. The new and living way

For since the law has but a shadow of the good things to come instead of the true form of these realities, it can never, by the same sacrifices which are continually offered year after year, make perfect those who draw near. Otherwise, would they not have ceased to be offered? If the worshippers had once been cleansed, they would no longer have any consciousness of sin. But in these sacrifices there is a reminder of sin year after year. For it is impossible that the blood of bulls and goats should take away sins....

And every priest stands daily at his service, offering repeatedly the same sacrifices, which can never take away sins. But when Christ had offered for all time a single sacrifice for sins, he sat down at the right hand of God, then to wait until his enemies should be made a stool for his feet. For by a single offering he has perfected for all time those who are sanctified. And the Holy Spirit also bears witness to us; for after saying,

'This is the covenant that I will make with them
after those days, says the Lord:
I will put my laws on their hearts,
and write them on their minds,'
then he adds,
'I will remember their sins and their misdeeds no more.'
Where there is forgiveness of these, there is no longer any offering for sin.

Therefore, brethren, since we have confidence to enter the sanctuary by the blood of Jesus, by the new and living way which he opened for us through the curtain, that is, through his flesh, and since we have a great priest over the house of God, let us draw near with a true heart in full assurance of faith, with our hearts sprinkled clean from an evil conscience and our bodies washed with pure water.

Hebrews 10:1–4, 11–22

Charles Simeon's conversion to Christ

'My distress of mind continued for about three months, and well might it have continued for years, since my sins were more in number than the hairs of my head; but God in infinite condescension began at last to smile upon me, and to give me a hope of acceptance with Him.

'But in Passion Week, as I was reading Bishop Wilson on the Lord's Supper, I met with an expression to this effect—"That the Jews knew what they did, when they transferred their sin to the head of their offering." The thought came into my mind, What, may I transfer all my guilt to another? Has God provided an Offering for me, that I may lay my sins on His head? Then, God willing, I will not bear them on my own soul one moment longer. Accordingly I sought to lay my sins upon the sacred head of Jesus; and on the Wednesday began to have a hope of mercy; on the Thursday that hope increased; on the Friday and Saturday it became more strong; and on the Sunday morning, Easterday, April 4, I awoke early with those words upon my heart and lips, "Jesus Christ is risen to-day! Hallelujah! Hallelujah!" From that hour peace flowed in rich abundance into my soul; and at the Lord's Table in our Chapel I had the sweetest access to God through my blessed Saviour. I remember on that occasion, there being more bread consecrated than was sufficient for the communicants, the clergyman gave some of us a piece more of it after the service; and on my putting it into my mouth, I covered my face with my hand and prayed. The clergyman seeing it smiled at me; but I thought, if he had felt such a load taken off from his soul as I did, and had been as sensible of his obligations to the Lord Jesus Christ as I was, he would not deem my prayers and praises at all superfluous.'

Quoted by H. C. G. Moule

As I enter your holy presence, Lord,
in this quiet room
I find it hard to imagine
the great temple, the smoking sacrifice,
the lambs and kids awaiting slaughter,
the knives, the blood, the solemn ceremony
of life poured out
to take away your people's sins.

What a hard lesson it must be for men to learn
if over many centuries
this was the way you showed yourself a holy God.
And so I thank you for this
new covenant; this new and living way.

It is, I recognize, still by blood.
I come, as they came, only by sacrifice.
But my Lamb of Sacrifice is Jesus.
Upon his sacred head I lay my sins.
        O Lord, my God and Father,
no wonder guilt lies heavy on the heart,
recognized or unrecognized,
of modern man!
If all that ritual of blood could never purge man's guilt,
but only point to Christ the Lamb of God,
how can any man be free of guilt
gnawing unnoticed in the secret places of his soul?

Only through Christ:
but perfectly through him.
He is the true and living way, the sin-bearer, and
the risen Saviour.
In him I rest and I rejoice.

Amen.

56. The highest price

And what more shall I say? For time would fail me to tell of Gideon, Barak, Samson, Jephthah, of David and Samuel and the prophets–who through faith conquered kingdoms, enforced justice, received promises, stopped the mouths of lions, quenched raging fire, escaped the edge of the sword, won strength out of weakness, became mighty in war, put foreign armies to flight. Women received their dead by resurrection. Some were tortured, refusing to accept release, that they might rise again to a better life. Others suffered mocking and scourging, and even chains and imprisonment. They were stoned, they were sawn in two, they were killed with the sword; they went about in skins of sheep and goats, destitute, afflicted, ill-treated—of whom the world was not worthy—wandering over deserts and mountains, and in dens and caves of the earth.

And all these, though well attested by their faith, did not receive what was promised, since God had foreseen something better for us, that apart from us they should not be made perfect.

Hebrews 11:32–39

A modern martyrdom

When I first met Miss Coplestone, in this room,
I saw the image, standing behind her chair,
Of a Celia Coplestone whose face showed the astonishment
Of the first five minutes after a violent death.
If this strains your credulity, Mrs Chamberlayne,
I ask you only to entertain the suggestion
That a sudden intuition, in certain minds,
May tend to express itself at once in a picture.
That happens to me, sometimes. So it was obvious
That here was a woman under sentence of death.
That was her destiny. The only question
Then was, what sort of death? *I* could not know;
Because it was for her to choose the way of life
To lead to death, and, without knowing the end
Yet choose the form of death. We know the death she chose
I did not know that she would die in this way;
She did not know. So all that I could do
Was to direct her in the way of preparation.
That way, which she accepted, led to this death.
And if that is not a happy death, what death is happy?
EDWARD. Do you mean that having chosen this form of death
She did not suffer as ordinary people suffer?
REILLY. Not at all what I mean. Rather the contrary.
I'd say that she suffered all that we should suffer
In fear and pain and loathing—all these together—
And reluctance of the body to become a *thing*.
I'd say she suffered more, because more conscious

126

Than the rest of us. She paid the highest price
In suffering. That is part of the design.
LAVINIA. Perhaps she had been through greater agony beforehand.
I mean—I know nothing of her last two years.
REILLY. That shows some insight on your part, Mrs Chamberlayne;
But such experience can only be hinted at
In myths and images. To speak about it
We talk of darkness, labyrinths, Minotaur terrors.
But that world does not take the place of this one.
Do you imagine that the Saint in the desert
With spiritual evil always at his shoulder
Suffered any less from hunger, damp, exposure,
Bowel trouble, and the fear of lions,
Cold of the night and heat of the day, than we should?

T. S. Eliot

Lord, what big people are your saints!
Or is it that we are most of us
so small?

I wonder what are the links, the connections,
between heroic faithfulness in crisis
—paying the highest price—
and faithfulness in my domesticated latter-day discipleship?
'As now, so then,' Hudson Taylor used to say:
What am I preparing now
in strength of will, habits of obedience, willingness to suffer,
if such a call came to me?

Such calls do come. They are there daily
in the newspapers, sometimes not far from home.
Courage, Lord, seems for them
an aspect of faith. To those who trust you
you give what is needed:
          with the danger
          will come the courage.

After all, Lord, you know all about it.
You are no stranger to 'the highest price'.
May your suffering evoke
my loving;
may my loving inspire true faithfulness;
not only for unknown tomorrows
but for today. Amen.

57. The light and the darkness

This is the message we have heard from him and proclaim to you, that God is light and in him is no darkness at all. If we say we have fellowship with him while we walk in darkness, we lie and do not live according to the truth; but if we walk in the light, as he is in the light, we have fellowship with one another, and the blood of Jesus his Son cleanses us from all sin. If we say we have no sin, we deceive ourselves, and the truth is not in us. If we confess our sins, he is faithful and just, and will forgive our sins and cleanse us from all unrighteousness. If we say we have not sinned, we make him a liar, and his word is not in us.

My little children, I am writing this to you so that you may not sin; but if any one does sin, we have an advocate with the Father, Jesus Christ the righteous; and he is the expiation for our sins, and not for ours only but also for the sins of the whole world.

1 John 1: 5—2: 2

The blotting out

If He pleases to forget anything, then He can forget it. And I think that is what He does with our sins—that is, after He has got them away from us, once we are clean from them altogether. It would be a dreadful thing if He forgot them before that....

Silence before the Judge

Think not about thy sin so as to make it either less or greater in thine own eyes. Bring it to Jesus and let Him show thee how vile a thing it is. And leave it to Him to judge thee, sure that He will judge thee justly; extenuating nothing, for He hath to cleanse thee utterly; and yet forgetting no smallest excuse that may cover the amazement of thy guilt or witness for thee that not with open eyes didst thou do the deed.... But again, I say, let it be Christ that excuseth thee. He will do it to more purpose than thou, and will not wrong thy soul by excusing thee a hair too much, or thy heart by excusing thee a hair to little.

The Mystery of Evil

The darkness knows neither the light nor itself; only the light knows itself and the darkness also. None but God hates evil and understands it.

George MacDonald

Lord Jesus Christ, you are the light
without whom darkness
would be over all the earth,
in every heart.
I come, Lord, to thank you for this light,
gladdening, healing, life-giving,
which shines in the darkness and is not
quenched by it.
    Thank you for such light, my Lord and my God.

And thank you, too, for light restored,
for forgiveness
when we have sinned against the light.
You see my sins as I shall never see them,
as they really are.
You see not only them but me;
me as I really am—
and yet forgive. 'The blood of Jesus Christ
goes on cleansing us from
all sin.'

And so again I turn to the light, to
your ever-waiting presence,
more ready to hear
than we to pray.
    I bring this sin ... and this ... this done,
and that not done. The thoughts and words and acts
said and not said, done and not done.
    I here confess them.
And abased, ashamed, truly sorry
for my sins, I claim your promise:
'If we confess our sins, you are faithful and just,
and will forgive our sins and cleanse us
from all unrighteousness.'
    Thank you.
Thank you for the light.
So let me walk in it.

Amen.

58. Shutting the door

And to the angel of the church in Laodicea write: "The words of the Amen, the faithful and true witness, the beginning of God's creation.

' "I know your works: you are neither cold nor hot. Would that you were cold or hot! So, because you are lukewarm, and neither cold nor hot, I will spew you out of my mouth. For you say, I am rich, I have prospered, and I need nothing; not knowing that you are wretched, pitiable, poor, blind, and naked. Therefore I counsel you to buy from me gold refined by fire, that you may be rich, and white garments to clothe you and to keep the shame of your nakedness from being seen, and salve to anoint your eyes, that you may see. Those whom I love, I reprove and chasten; so be zealous and repent. Behold, I stand at the door and knock, if any one hears my voice and opens the door, I will come in to him and eat with him, and he with me. He who conquers, I will grant him to sit with me on my throne, as I myself conquered and sat down with my Father on his throne. He who has an ear, let him hear what the Spirit says to the churches." '

Revelation 3: 14–22

In sight of Trebizond

Later in the morning, when I was on deck looking through glasses for the first sight of Trebizond, he came and stood by me and said, 'How much longer are you going on like this, shutting the door against God?'

This question always disturbed me; I sometimes asked it of myself, but I did not know the answer. Perhaps it would have to be for always, because I was so deeply committed to something else that I could not break away.

'I don't know,' I said.

'It's your business to know. There is no question. You must decide at once. Do you mean to drag on for years more in deliberate sin, refusing grace, denying the Holy Spirit? And when it ends, what then? It will end; such things always end. What then? Shall you come back, when it is taken out of your hands and it will cost you nothing? When you will have nothing to offer to God but a burnt-out fire and a fag end? Oh, he'll take it, he'll take anything we offer. It is you who will be impoverished for ever by so poor a gift. Offer now what will cost you a great deal, and you'll be enriched beyond anything you can imagine. How do you know how much of life you still have? It may be many years, it may be a few weeks. You may leave this world without grace, go on into the next stage in the chains you won't break now. Do you ever think of that, or have you put yourself beyond caring?'

Not quite, never quite. I had tried, but never quite. From time to time I knew what I had lost. But nearly all the time, God was a bad second, enough to hurt but not to cure, to hide from but not to seek, and I knew that when I died I should hear him saying. "Go away, I never knew you," and that would be the end of it all, the end of everything, and after that I never should know him, though then to

know him would be what I should want more than anything, and not to
know him would be hell.

Rose Macaulay

Lord, is this me?
Not perhaps 'shutting the door
against God' but less than
whole-hearted; making of you, Lord
a bad second
in my order of priorities?
(No need to ask who comes an easy first.)
Lord, is this me?

I suppose in some sense it must be.
Indeed, in some sense it must be
all of us.

And saying this, my Lord and Saviour, I recall
when first I heard your voice,
your knock;
and opened that shut door to take you at your word.
As the years pass I ask myself
—and I ask you to show me—
whether my fellowship has deepened, my love matured,
or whether I have indeed
grown cold—a burnt-out fire?

One thing I know:
your love remains the same.
Make it then, if there is no other way,
a chastening love leading towards repentance,
rekindling love in me.

What a lot of words, Lord Jesus,
for a simple prayer!
Be Master of my house,
its hearth and warmth,
its light and sun,
its feast and comfort,
its purpose and its joy:
for your Name's sake. Amen.

59. A wearied spirit

Then one of the elders addressed me, saying, 'Who are these, clothed in white robes, and whence have they come?' I said to him, 'Sir, you know.' And he said to me, 'These are they who have come out of the great tribulation; they have washed their robes and made them white in the blood of the Lamb.
Therefore are they before the throne of God,
and serve him day and night within his temple;
and he who sits upon the throne will shelter them with his presence.
They shall hunger no more, neither thirst any more;
the sun shall not strike them, nor any scorching heat.
For the Lamb in the midst of the throne will be their shepherd,
and he will guide them to springs of living water;
and God will wipe away every tear from their eyes.'

Revelation 7:13–17

O come quickly!

Never weather-beaten sail more willing bent to shore,
Never tired pilgrim's limbs affected slumber more,
Than my wearied sprite now longs to fly out of my troubled breast—
O come quickly, sweetest Lord, and take my soul to rest!

Ever blooming are the joys of heaven's high Paradise,
Cold age deafs not there our ears, nor vapour dims our eyes:
Glory there the sun outshines, whose beams the Blessed only see—
O come quickly, glorious Lord, and raise my sprite to Thee!

Thomas Campion

I wonder which is worse?
—worse to you, O my God—that I should
feel like weeping, and that I should have no tears:
or not even to feel in the face of sorrow?
        Sometimes, as you well know,
I'm past all feeling:
too proud, too hard,
too self-contained—too lazy even—to allow
myself to feel.
And yet I know this feeling: the weatherbeaten sail,
the weary pilgrim, the aching
longing
of a human spirit sick for home.

And what a home!
        'Glory there the sun outshines,'
        'They shall hunger no more,
        neither thirst any more'
        'And he who sits on the throne will shelter them with
        his presence'.
Will shelter me! Will be my shepherd!
        'And God will wipe away every tear'

Lord, give me tears, real, heartfelt, secret,
genuine;
for this world, for my brothers, for my own lovelessness
and sinfulness.
And when I have learned to weep for others,
then 'Come quickly, glorious Lord',
that by the blood of the Lamb
I find my home in heaven.
For Jesus' sake.

Amen.

60. 'There is a country...'

And I saw no temple in the city, for its temple is the Lord God the Almighty and the Lamb. And the city has no need of sun or moon to shine upon it, for the glory of God is its light, and its lamp is the Lamb. By its light shall the nations walk; and the kings of the earth shall bring their glory into it, and its gates shall never be shut by day —and there shall be no night there; they shall bring into it the glory and the honour of the nations. But nothing unclean shall enter it, nor any one who practises abomination or falsehood, but only those who are written in the Lamb's book of life.

Then he showed me the river of the water of life, bright as crystal, flowing from the throne of God and of the Lamb through the middle of the street of the city; also, on either side of the river, the tree of life with its twelve kinds of fruit, yielding its fruit each month; and the leaves of the tree were for the healing of the nations. There shall no more be anything accursed, but the throne of God and of the Lamb shall be in it, and his servants shall worship him; they shall see his face, and his name shall be on their foreheads. And night shall be no more; they need no light of lamp or sun, for the Lord God will be their light, and they shall reign for ever and ever.

Revelation 21: 22–22: 5

Peace

My soul, there is a country
    Afar beyond the stars,
Where stands a wingèd sentry
    All skilful in the wars.
There, above noise and danger,
    Sweet peace sits crowned with smiles,
And One born in a manger
    Commands the beauteous files.
He is thy gracious friend
    And (O my soul awake)
Did in pure love descend,
    To die here for thy sake.
If thou canst get but thither,
    There grows the flower of peace,
The rose that cannot wither,
    Thy fortress, and thy ease.
Leave then thy foolish ranges;
    For none can thee secure,
But One who never changes,
    Thy God, thy Life, thy Cure.

Henry Vaughan

Heaven, my God?

Can it be right to think of heaven,
with so much hell on earth?

So much to do, so little time.
But this will be a busy, fretful day: I have a feeling
that it may turn out to be
'one of those days'.
So I drink of the peace you offer: I rest
my eyes on the vision of heaven, where grows
the flower of peace.

A flower, who knows?
But a river certainly,
deep and clear and bright and cool,
the water of life.

Now, as the day starts
I drink that water, sparkling with the light of heaven,
laden with life-giving powers from the throne of God.
    No sun or moon,
    no night, no lamp,
    no church or temple,
    no evil, falsehood or decay,
but 'one who never changes'—
that is, you, my God.

And where you are is heaven.
This day is heaven then for me
till that day comes.

Amen.